High-Intensity Bodybuilding

by Ellington Darden, Ph.D. • Photography by Chris Lund

Scott Wilson displays the muscle-building effects of super high-intensity curls.

A Perigee Book

OTHER BOOKS OF INTEREST
BY ELLINGTON DARDEN, PH.D.
The Nautilus Bodybuilding Book (Revised Edition)
The Nautilus Book (Revised Edition)
The Nautilus Woman (Revised Edition)
The Nautilus Nutrition Book
The Nautilus Advanced Bodybuilding Book
The Athlete's Guide to Sports Medicine
Strength-Training Principles
Conditioning for Football
The Nautilus Diet
High-Intensity Bodybuilding

For a free catalog of bodybuilding books, please send a self-addressed, stamped envelope to Dr. Ellington Darden, Darden Research Corporation, PO Box 1016, Lake Helen, FL 32744.

WARNING!
The high-intensity routines in this book are intended only for healthy men and women. People with health problems should not follow these routines without a physician's approval. Before beginning any exercise or dietary program, always consult with your doctor.

ACKNOWLEDGMENTS
Special appreciation is extended to the following gyms: Gold's Gym of Venice, California; World Gym of Santa Monica, California; Champion's Gym of Hamilton, Ontario; and Gilmore's Gym of DeLand, Florida.

Perigee Books, a division of
G. P. Putnam's Sons
Publishers Since 1838
200 Madison Avenue
New York, NY 10016

Book design by
Martin Moskof Associates

Copyright © 1986 by Ellington Darden
All rights reserved. This book, or parts thereof, may not be reproduced in any form without permission.
Published simultaneously in Canada by
General Publishing Co. Limited, Toronto

Library of Congress Cataloging-in-Publication Data
Darden, Ellington (1943-)
Super high-intensity bodybuilding.
1. Bodybuilding I. Title
GV546.5.D38 1986   646.7'5   85-21665
ISBN 0-399-51220-9

Printed in the United States of America
6 7 8 9 10

Lee Haney, Mr. Olympia of 1984 and 1985, contracts his high-intensity triceps.

Contents

CHAPTER 1

Muscles:
Renewing Growth by
Not Overtraining

Page 8

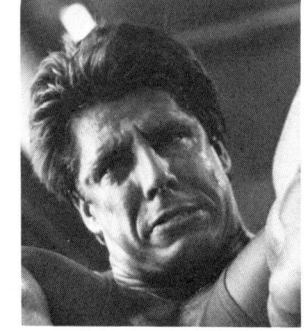

CHAPTER 2

Recovery:
Making the Most of
an Ignored Factor

Page 20

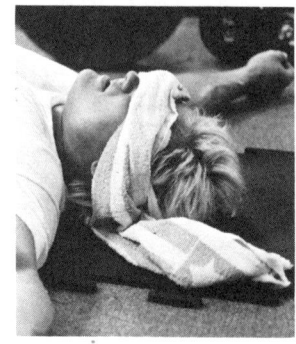

CHAPTER 3

Techniques:
Understanding
Super High-Intensity

Page 34

CHAPTER 4

Thighs:
Discovering an Old
Method of Squatting

Page 52

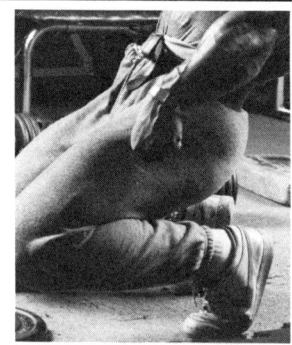

CHAPTER 5

Calves:
Building
Diamond-Shaped
Lower Legs

Page 66

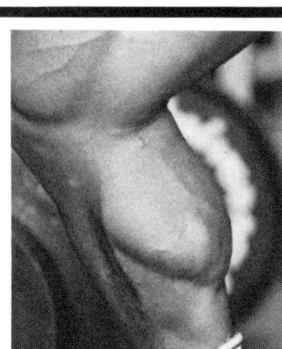

CHAPTER 6

Back:
Creating Thickness
in Your Lats

Page 74

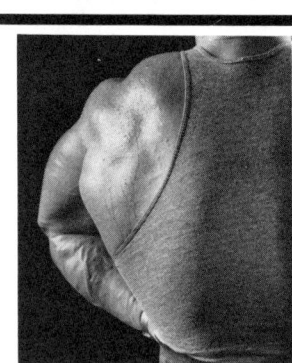

CHAPTER 7

Shoulders:
Widening
the Triangle

Page 86

CHAPTER 8

Chest:
Developing
Powerful Pectorals

Page 98

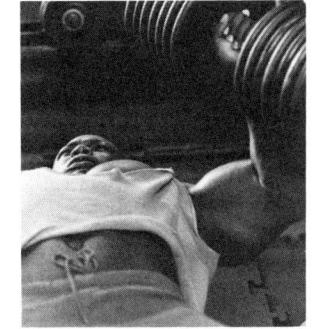

CHAPTER 9

Arms:
Concentrating on Your
Biceps and Triceps

Page 110

CHAPTER 10

Forearms:
Getting a Grip on
Massive Development

Page 126

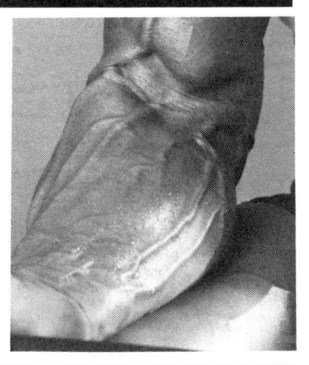

CHAPTER 11

Lower Back:
Thickening Your
Spinal Erectors

Page 138

CHAPTER 12

Waist:
Ripping
Your Abdominals

Page 146

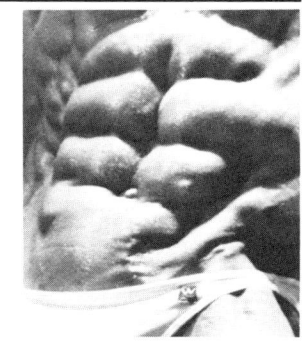

CHAPTER 13

Neck:
Expanding
Your Collar

Page 160

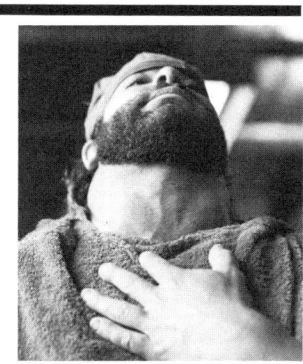

CHAPTER 14

Problems:
Answering
Your Questions

Page 172

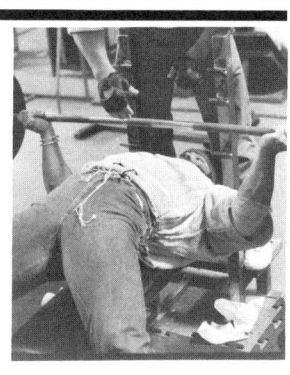

CONCLUSION

Believe!
Super High-Intensity
Bodybuilding
Is the Way!

Page 188

CHAPTER 1
SUPER HIGH-INTENSITY BODYBUILDING

To renew the muscular growth process, you must avoid overtraining. The secret is to train harder, but more briefly.

Muscles: Renewing Growth by Not Overtraining

"Help! My muscles aren't growing."
"I've reached a plateau."
"I'm not making progress."

I frequently hear comments like these from frustrated bodybuilders. The solution to their lack of progress can often be stated in two words: *quit overtraining*. Overtraining stops muscular growth cold in its tracks. Overtraining makes progress impossible or, at best, slow.

Overtraining Examined

The concept of overtraining was first introduced to me by Nautilus developer Arthur Jones. I met Jones at the 1970 Mr. USA contest in New Orleans. Casey Viator won the contest, and Jones had been training him for a month prior to the event. I was very impressed with Viator's mass and muscularity. At the same time I was displeased with my own training and the results I was getting.

"At a glance I can tell your body's in a state of overtraining," Jones said to me, after the contest.

Jones might be right, I thought to myself. Prior to the Mr. USA contest I was exercising on a six-day-a-week split routine. Each of my workouts lasted one and a half hours, so I was spending nine hours per week in the gym.

"Drive down to DeLand, Florida," challenged Jones, "and I'll show you the efficient way to muscular growth."

DeLand was 225 miles south of Tallahassee, where I was enrolled in graduate school at Florida State University, but several months later I did visit Jones and got a chance to exercise under his supervision. His brief, high-intensity training was drastically different from what I had been used to doing. The workout was simple, but very demanding.

I returned to Tallahassee with rekindled enthusiasm and immediately began applying the concepts that Jones had discussed with me. Instead of training six days a week, I reduced my workouts to four days a week. My weekly time in the gym went from nine hours to six hours. As a result, my body started growing—for a while. Then, rather than reduce my workouts even further, I gradually started training more. My progress stopped, and once again my body started feeling the effects of overtraining. At that time, I couldn't fully understand what was happening. That took another eight months. Jones's concepts were still salient in my mind, but I just wasn't sure how to utilize them.

On May 16, 1971, Jones entered Casey Viator in the Jr. Mr. America contest. He had now personally trained him on and off for almost ten months. Viator won with ease. Four weeks later, on June 12, 1971, Casey entered and won the Mr. America title in the most spectacular fashion in the history of such contests. In addition to the Mr. America title, Viator won the subdivisions for Most Muscular, Best Arms, Best Back, Best Chest, and Best Legs—all at nineteen years of age!

More than thirty of the leading bodybuilders in the country competed against Viator for the title. The meaningful discovery from Jones's viewpoint was that all of them were probably overtrained. They all trained at least six times a week, or at least twenty-four times, during the four weeks immediately prior to the contest. They were making the identical mistake that I had made—and was still making.

Casey, on the other hand, trained a total of *six times* during the same four weeks. He didn't train at all for the two weeks after the Jr. Mr. America. And he trained only three times weekly during the two weeks before the Mr. America contest. The workouts were not split into the traditional upper body one day and lower body the next day; each one was designed for the total body. Each session lasted one hour or less, which meant his weekly training time totaled no more than three hours.

Casey's Routine

On the night of June 10, 1971, two days before the Mr. America contest, I personally witnessed Casey Viator perform the following leg routine:

1. Leg press on Universal machine, 750 pounds, for twenty repetitions, immediately followed by
2. Leg extension on Universal machine, 225 pounds for twenty repetitions, immediately followed by
3. Full squat with barbell, 502 pounds for thirteen repetitions.

REST FOR TWO MINUTES.

4. Leg curl on Universal machine, 175 pounds for twelve repetitions, reduce weight to 150 pounds

---

Arthur Jones, the inventor of Nautilus equipment, is the driving force behind the high-intensity approach to bodybuilding.
Overleaf. **Casey Viator, at age nineteen, contracts his mighty biceps, several months before he won the 1971 Mr. America title.**

for ten repetitions, immediately followed by
5. One-legged calf raise with 40-pound dumbbell held in one hand, first one leg and then the other, for three sets of fifteen repetitions for each leg.

Jones pushed Viator through each exercise, and every set was carried to the point of momentary muscular failure. With the exception of the two-minute rest period after the squats, there was no rest between sets. Viator's entire leg routine was over in eleven minutes.

Casey's upper body routine was as follows:

6. Pullover on Nautilus machine, 400 pounds for eleven repetitions, immediately followed by
7. Behind neck on Nautilus machine, 200 pounds for ten repetitions, immediately followed by
8. Rowing on Nautilus machine, 200 pounds for ten repetitions, immediately followed by
9. Behind neck pulldown on Nautilus machine, 210 pounds for ten repetitions.

REST FOR TWO MINUTES.

10. Straight-armed lateral raise with dumbbells, 40 pounds in each hand for nine repetitions, immediately followed by
11. Press behind neck with barbell, 185 pounds for ten repetitions.

REST FOR TWO MINUTES.

12. Biceps curl on Nautilus plateloading machine, 110 pounds for eight repetitions, immediately followed by
13. Chin-up, bodyweight for twelve repetitions.

REST FOR ONE MINUTE.

14. Triceps extension on Nautilus plateloading machine, 125 pounds for nine repetitions, immediately followed by
15. Parallel dip, bodyweight for twenty-two repetitions.

Viator's upper body workout on the night of June 10, 1971, was finished in seventeen minutes and forty seconds. His entire workout, from walking into the gym to walking out, which included rest periods, water breaks, and several minutes of posing at the end, took forty-one minutes.

High-Intensity Applications

After observing Viator's workout and talking more with Jones about his concepts, I returned to Tallahassee and decided to give high-intensity training

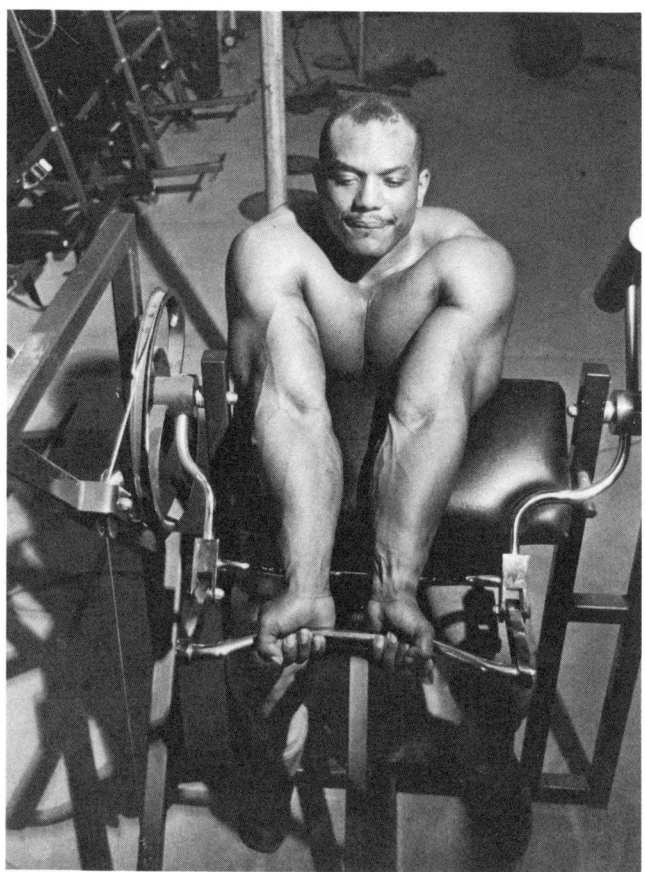

Above. The huge arms of Sergio Oliva are shown in the stretched position of the Nautilus biceps machine. Sergio was trained by Arthur Jones during the summer of 1971.

A series of 1971 training shots of Casey Viator going through an intensive workout. *Below.* Squat. *Opposite, left.* Curl. *Opposite, below right.* Leg extension.

Opposite, above right. Arnold Schwarzenegger uses an early model of a Nautilus pullover machine. Arnold spent several days with Arthur Jones during the spring of 1971.

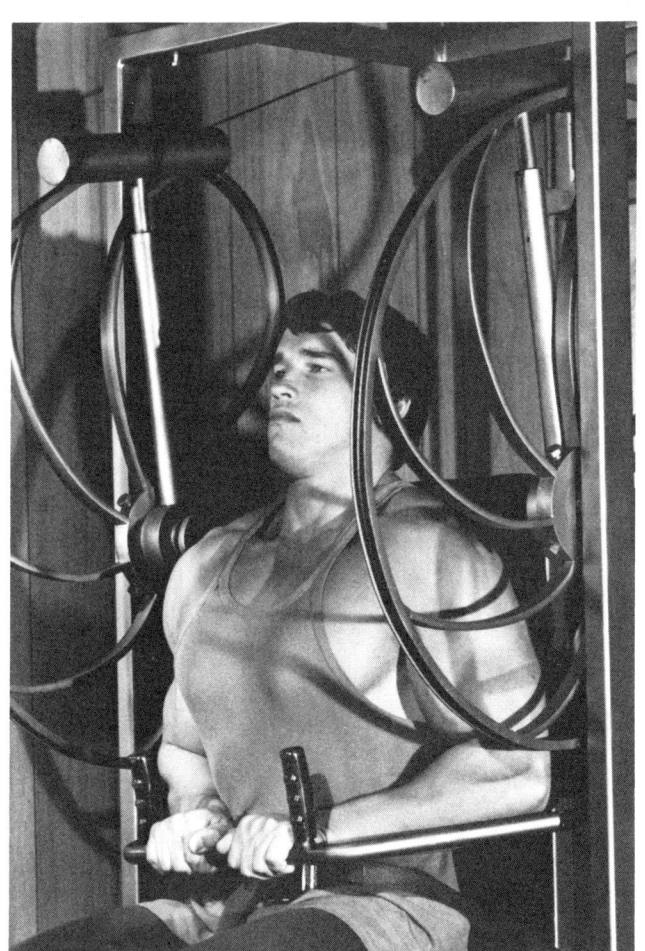

15

another try. Here's what I did:

1. Trained my entire body during each workout.
2. Selected only twelve basic exercises to perform.
3. Performed each exercise in a high-intensity manner, or until no additional repetitions were possible.
4. Limited each exercise to two sets.
5. Repeated the workouts three times per week.

I trained harder than I had previously. It took me four sessions to finally make it through two sets of twelve exercises. For the first three workouts the intensity of the exercise would make me feel nauseated after fifteen to twenty minutes. Once I got my body accustomed to high-intensity training, I could understand why Jones said: "You cannot stand much in the way of high-intensity exercise. It must be brief and infrequent."

After another month of three-times-per-week training, my bodyweight was up five pounds and my muscular size and strength were increasing steadily. I was pleased, and decided to drive to DeLand and visit with Arthur Jones once again.

Observing my results, Jones recommended that I reduce my workouts even further. "Do two sets of ten exercises," he suggested, "and you'll get even better results. Then, after several months when you reach another sticking point, reduce your routine to two sets of eight exercises."

"But Arthur," I asked, "with sixteen sets, will I be getting enough exercise?"

"Don't knock it until you've tried it," he replied. "I guarantee it will be enough, if you use as much weight as you can and if you perform all the exercises in perfect form and carry each set to a point of failure."

Jones was right! Six months later, I was in the best shape of my life. As a result, in April 1972 I entered and won the Collegiate Mr. America contest.

Although my physique was never in the same category as Casey Viator's (he had much more genetic potential than I did), I feel I reached a high level of body development and symmetry for my bone structure and muscular potential. And in the process, I learned a great deal about efficient bodybuilding. Although I haven't entered a bodybuilding contest since 1972, I haven't lost interest in my training or the sport.

After finishing a Ph.D. in physical education at Florida State University, I moved to the DeLand area in 1973 and went to work for Arthur Jones and Nautilus Sports/Medical Industries. While serving as Director of Research for Nautilus, I've spent hundreds of hours listening, questioning, and discussing muscle building with Jones. That has provided me with a rare education. Furthermore, I've spent thousands of hours training athletes who were interested in attaining high levels of muscular size and strength. Such experience puts me on solid ground to write this book.

But, as Arthur Jones frequently notes: "Bodybuilders usually make two common mistakes—some think that intelligence is a substitute for experience, and some think that experience is a substitute for intelligence. To build your body efficiently you need both intelligence and experience."

Experience and intelligence reveal that brief and infrequent training is an absolute requirement for the best possible results from exercise. Yet almost all currently active bodybuilders devote to their workouts several times as much weekly training time as is necessary, while producing little in the way of results for their efforts.

Reducing Training Time by 50 Percent

If each bodybuilder in this country suddenly cut his or her training in half—merely reduced weekly workouts by 50 percent, while making no other change in training—it is my belief that overall results would be at least doubled.

Overtraining is so common that such a 50 percent reduction on the part of all bodybuilders would result in an immediate improvement in the rates of progress being experienced by most trainees—an improvement that would probably double average overall results. And since such doubled results would be produced by only half as much training, the rate of progress would be quadrupled—a four-to-one improvement.

Since a few bodybuilders are now training properly, these few would suffer from a reduction in their training time. But for every individual presently training right, there are probably a hundred training wrong—and usually overtraining. Thus for each bodybuilder who lost from such reduction in training time, a hundred would gain—and on the average, the overall results would be strongly positive.

If, in addition to the overall average reduction in training suggested in the example above, everybody simultaneously started training properly insofar as *intensity of effort* is concerned, then at least another doubling of average results would be produced. The average rate of progress, therefore, would be increased from its present level by a ratio of approximately eight to one.

If this point is understood and put into practical application, then a long first step will have been taken in the direction of sensible bodybuilding.

Importance of Harder, Briefer Exercise

Barbell exercises are more productive than freehand exercises for only one reason: Barbell exercises are *harder* than nonweighted exercises. But as you increase the *intensity* of an exercise, it is necessary to reduce the *amount* of exercise. Japanese Sumo wrestlers do as many as three thousand repetitions of free-hand squats almost daily. Try doing that many squats with a heavy barbell and see what happens.

I do not want to suggest that at Nautilus we have tried literally *everything* or that we fully understand all of the

---

Ellington Darden won the Collegiate Mr. America title in 1972, while attending graduate school at Florida State University.

factors involved, but we have tried a lot of things under carefully controlled conditions and with hundreds of trainees. The evidence always points to the same basic conclusions: more than three weekly workouts, or more than three sets of any one exercise in the same workout, or more than a total of three hours of weekly training will almost always result in overtraining.

Renewing Growth

The cornerstone of building larger, stronger muscles, especially for advanced trainees, is to *quit overtraining*. Or, said another way, the secret to renewing the muscular growth process is to *avoid overtraining*.

To avoid overtraining requires that workouts be very brief, but very hard. And that's precisely the subject of this book. *Super High-Intensity Bodybuilding* is not for beginners. It is for advanced bodybuilders, only—advanced bodybuilders who are not afraid of hard, brief work.

If the primary guidelines covered in this and later chapters are clearly understood, then almost any reasonably intelligent bodybuilder will have the knowledge required for renewing growth and for getting maximum results from training.

A Visit from Arnold Schwarzenegger

Shortly after Casey Viator won the 1971 Mr. America contest, Arnold Schwarzenegger and Franco Columbu, both Mr. Olympia winners, spent several days in Florida visiting Arthur Jones. Naturally, they observed Viator training.

When Arnold returned to California, he wrote an article about Casey that was later published in *Muscle Builder* (June 1972). Arnold did an interesting job of describing what only a few people ever witnessed:

> Viator is a gym monster. I never witnessed such ferocious, almost suicidal training in my life. He kills the weights. He mangles the equipment. And most of all he tortures himself to hysteria. . . .
>
> He does forced reps until an observer could puke from horror. He absolutely torments himself; he turns blue in the face. He pumps so much blood into an attacked muscle it looks like a minizeppelin. Each set is blasted past failure exactly the same way. The muscles are never shown any mercy whatsoever. They expand 200 percent . . . 300 percent. More. Not only that, but when a set ends, no rest. Next exercise in a flash. . . .
>
> He switches from movement to movement. From apparatus to apparatus faster than you could take notes. He bangs away at each set until he can't muster another muscle twitch. He flushes each body part until the limb or area is paralyzed. This is prime quality multiplied by a factor of dedication and madness no bodybuilder has ever approached. If I had to do this every day I'd opt for a hernia, go back to Austria and be a ski instructor.

What Arnold observed and so richly described, he still failed to understand. His last sentence, which I've paraphrased, tells all: "If I had to train every day the way Viator does, I'd quit and go back to Austria." It would be *impossible* to train the way Viator does *every day*. And trying to do so, as Jones occasionally says, would "kill a large male gorilla!"

Remember, Viator himself could train with such ferocity only three times a week. And even three times a week would soon have to be reduced to twice a week to get the best possible growth stimulation while avoiding overtraining.

Left. **Tom Platz, a former Mr. Universe winner, understands the importance of harder, briefer workouts.**
Opposite, above. **Franco Columbu & Casey Viator compare upper arms before an Arthur Jones training session.**
Opposite, below. **"Viator is a gym monster," said Arnold the first time he watched Casey train.**

Some Symptoms of Overtraining

If you have *any* of these symptoms, you are probably overtraining:

1. No training progress
2. Decreased muscle size and strength
3. Longer-than-average recovery time after a workout
4. Increased heart rate
5. Increased blood pressure
6. Increased joint and muscle aches
7. Loss of interest in training
8. Lack of energy
9. Headaches
10. Hand tremors
11. Loss or diminution of appetite
12. Tiredness
13. Irritability
14. Listlessness
15. Insomnia

CHAPTER 2
SUPER HIGH-INTENSITY BODYBUILDING

Your muscles grow not when you are training, but when you are resting.

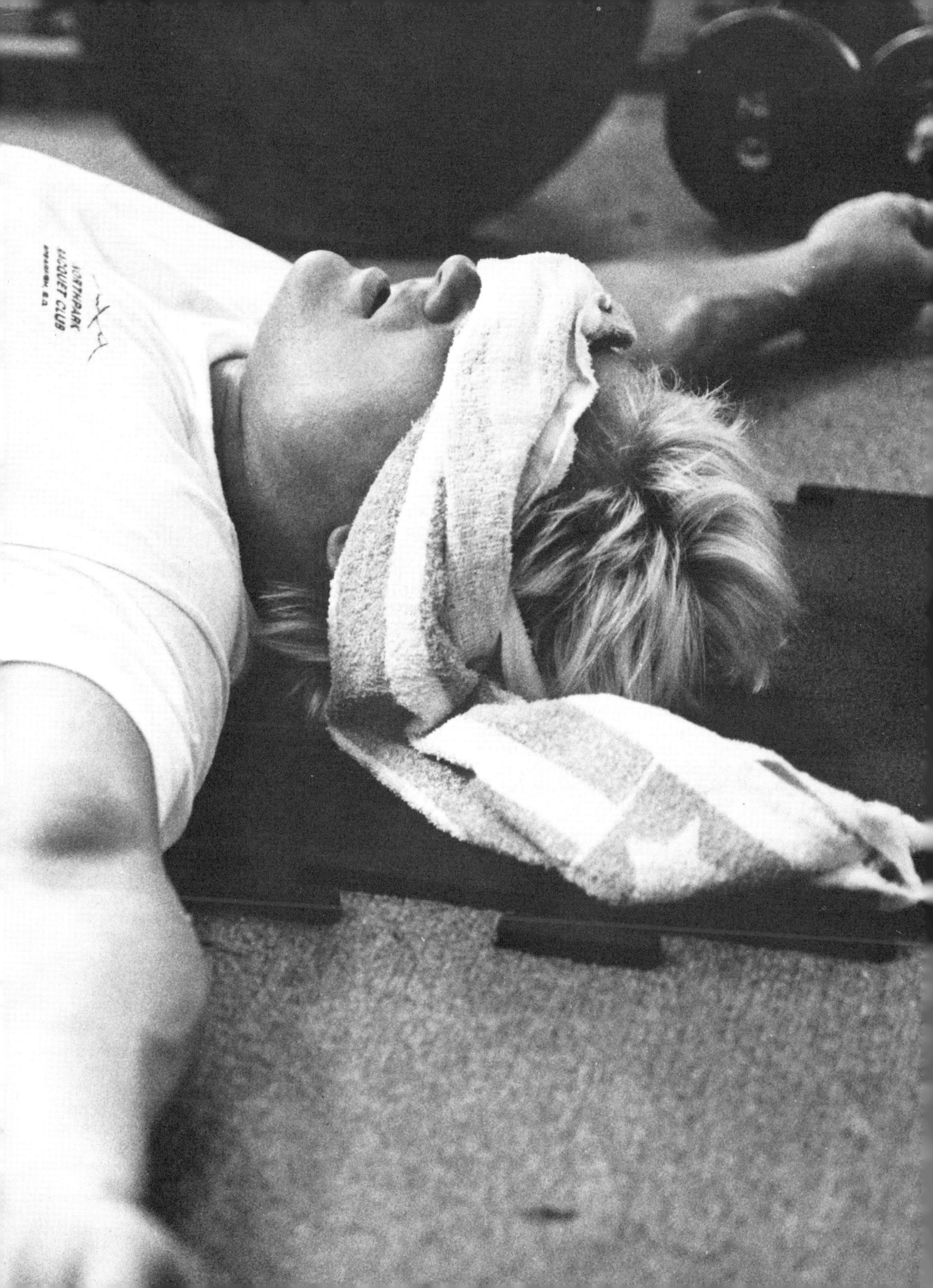

Recovery:
Making the Most of an Ignored Factor

Your personal training does only three things—and two of the three are bad.

First, exercise stimulates your body to grow larger and stronger. Second, exercise beyond the minimum amount for stimulation prevents optimum growth by depleting your body of energy. Third, exercise, if done improperly, produces injury.

All the worthwhile results from exercise are produced by your body. It adapts, it improves, it grows. Exercise does not produce these gains. It merely stimulates your body to produce them. Injury, not growth, remains the only direct result of exercise.

The key factors in muscular growth are *stimulation* and *overcompensation*. Stimulation is the result of high-intensity training, which is the overall subject of this book. Overcompensation is primarily related to your body's recovery ability.

Recovery Ability Defined

Recovery ability can be defined as the chemical reactions that are necessary for your body to produce muscular growth. Although this entire process is very complicated and still not completely understood, it includes the producing and mixing of such chemicals as hydrogen, oxygen, phosphate, adenosine triphosphate, lactic acid, potassium, glycine, arginine, methionine, creatine, and creatine phosphate. An efficient recovery ability is dependent on adequate rest, balanced nutrition, and, most important, *time*.

Your recovery ability does not increase in proportion to your strength. The stronger you become, the more resistance you can handle on each exercise, and the demands you make on your recovery ability become greater. Thus, your body needs harder but briefer exercise for continued growth stimulation. It also needs longer rest periods after the workouts for efficient recovery.

A Practical Example

In 1971, Chuck Amato, a well-known Oregon bodybuilder who had won fifth palce in the 1970 Mr. America contest, spent almost two weeks in DeLand training under the guidance of Arthur Jones. The first thing Amato did was to rest—literally, do nothing—for four days. Amato had been on a steady training schedule for two years, and Jones knew his recovery ability needed rejuvenation.

Jones then trained him in a hard, brief manner four times over the next nine days. The results were almost unbelievable!

In nine days, Chuck Amato gained seven pounds of bodyweight, improved his existing degree of muscularity, added $13/16$ of an inch to his cold upper arm measurement and $3/4$ of an inch to his calves, and increased his curling strength by 50 percent.

The amazing thing is that Amato's two years of steady training, which averaged fifteen hours a week, had produced by his own admittance, "no visible results." During the nine-day period under Jones's supervision, Amato trained only four hours, but the results were spectacular.

Hard, brief training was an important factor, but of equal importance was his *well-rested recovery ability*.

Recovery and Energy

The first thing your body does following a workout is attempt to recover the energy it lost during the workout. If it is successful in doing so, and if you have trained hard enough to stimulate muscle growth, then any extra reserve you have will contribute toward growth. If you spend too much of your energy training in the gym, as with the six-day-a-week routines, then your body will expend all of its chemistry in an attempt to overcome the exhaustive effects of the workout. Nothing will be left over for growth.

Any amount of training—whether short or long—is always a negative factor, in that it drains some of your resources. The less you disturb your recovery ability, the more you will have available for growth. Marathon training—the six-day-a-week variety—is of insufficient intensity to stimulate much in the way of growth. It tears down your chemical reserves so much that none are left for growth. Hard, high-intensity training, on the other hand, has proven to be an actual requirement for growth. As it does not allow for long periods of training, there is more energy for growth once it has been stimulated.

The Effects of Physical Stress

This whole issue might be made more clear if we looked at it in terms of the body's capacity to cope with stress. While we are exposed to numerous forms of stress, both internally and externally, we can all relate to three forms of physical stress. They are the stress of

---

A beautiful, artistic pose by Joy Nichols of Canada.

the sun to the skin, abrasive friction to the skin, and intense activity to the muscles.

Up to a certain point, exposure to the sun will lead to the formation of a tan. Once you go past that rather definite point, however, and continue to expose the skin for too long a period, blisters form instead. Carried to ridiculous extremes, death will result. The tan is the result of a compensatory buildup process whereby the body protects itself in anticipation of stress in the future. Beyond that exposure time, the body is no longer able to cope with the stress of the sun. Burning therefore occurs.

The formation of a callus is much the same. The skin on the palm of the hand is generally much tougher than the rest of your skin, due to its greater direct contact with rough objects. The handling of abrasive objects, such as the knurling on a barbell, subjects the skin on the palms to high friction. If the friction is intense enough, the formation of a callus is stimulated. Then, if the amount of friction does not exceed a certain amount, a callus will form. Too much intense friction will cause a blister to develop, and, carried even further, the skin will begin to wear away altogether.

Here again, as is the case with the sun, the stress of the friction will lead to a compensatory buildup of extra skin that will protect the body from depletion when exposed to the same stress in the future. Carried to extremes, however, the body isn't able to build up the callus rapidly enough, and the constant friction keeps tearing it down as it forms.

Heavy barball and dumbbell training can be examined in much the same light. Intense exercise is a form of stress to the muscles and the overall physical system. Intense exercise, when not performed to excess, stimulates a compensatory buildup in the form of added muscle tissue, which aids the body in coping more successfully with similar stress in the future. Taken to extremes—as is the case with the training practices of most bodybuilders—the drain on the chemical subsystems of the body actually prevents the buildup of muscle. All of the reserves are spent in an attempt to overcome the depletion caused by overtraining.

Less Is Better!

These facts strongly suggest that the less time you spend in the gym, the better. Once you have stimulated growth with high-intensity exercise, then get out of the gym! Not only is any extra exercise not needed, it is actually counterproductive, needlessly draining more of the body's resources—resources that could have contributed to more growth. Even though there is a natural tendency to think "more is better," you must consciously fight that tendency if you wish to make the most rapid progress possible.

Many bodybuilding superstars do train six days a week for up to four hours a day. It does not necessarily follow that such methods were totally responsible for the physiques they developed. The top bodybuilders all possess a much higher than average tolerance to physical stress. Through a genetic advantage, they are better able to "overtrain" with less of a drain on their

Above. A 1971 photo of Chuck Amato and Casey Viator after an exercise session.
Opposite. Mr. Olympia Lee Haney takes a break from his workout.
Overleaf. Mr. Universe Bertil Fox and his training partner take a light break from some heavy exercise.

systems. Had they trained with higher intensity, which in turn would lead to less training, they would either have developed their physiques further, or they would have attained their development sooner.

Marathon Training—Not Worth the Price

Some respected authorities in bodybuilding have stated that it is impossible to gain more than eight pounds of pure muscle a year. That may very well be the case for someone who trains six days a week for two to four hours per workout. Considering the enormous drain on the body by such training, one would be lucky to gain even four pounds of muscle a year. This leads to a very interesting thought: If a person were to train two hours a day for six days a week, in a year he would have spent a total of 624 hours working out— and all for only eight pounds of muscle.

Many bodybuilders train twice that much—as much as four hours a day for six days a week, or 1,248 hours a year. Why? It hardly seems worth it! Imagine what a person could accomplish if he devoted that much time to attaining a college degree or earning a million dollars! The overenthusiasm that leads to such ill-conceived and irrational training methods is the very factor responsible for so many bodybuilding failures.

Recovery Aids

All bodybuilders should take measures to increase and preserve their valuable recovery abilities. The following guidelines can help.

1. _Stop overtraining_: As stated in the last chapter, one secret to renewing the muscular growth process is to conquer your desire for overtraining. Make sure that all of the time you spend in the gym is spent on intense, result-producing training. If you are training as hard as possible, then there is no need to spend more than an hour exercising. The needless repetition of "easy" tasks leads to serious overtraining, which drains your recovery ability. Remember, if you expend all of your energy and resources in the gym, then you will have nothing left for growth.

2. _Get adequate rest_: After a full day of activity, your body requires time to replenish and restore your spent energy supplies. Sleep requirements usually vary with individuals; make sure that you get enough sleep every night, however long it happens to be. Too little sleep leads to a further depletion of vital chemistry and hence a slow down in progress.

3. _Eat a balanced diet_: Since physical exercise is a form of stress that taxes your chemical resources, ample attention must be paid to the food that will replenish them. Nothing bordering on any form of fanaticism in nutrition is required for enhancing your recov-

---

Cory Everson and Rachel McLish as they looked at the 1984 Ms. Olympia contest.
Overleaf. **An informal shot of Gold's Gym in Venice, California.**

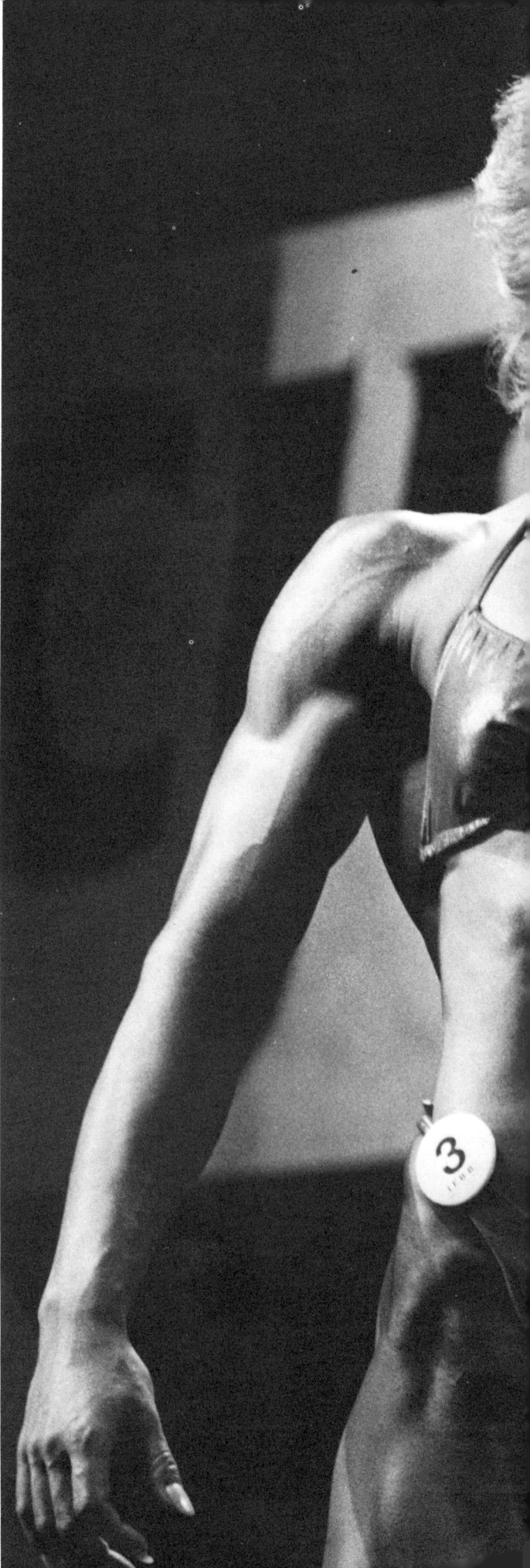

ery ability. All that is necessary is a balanced diet composed of approximately 55 percent carbohydrates, 30 percent fats, and 15 percent proteins. This can be supplied easily by several servings a day from the Basic Four Food Groups: meats, dairy products, fruits and vegetables, and breads and cereals. Contrary to what is said in most muscle magazines, special food supplements, such as vitamin pills, protein tablets, liquid amino acids, and glandular extracts, are not required for maximum recovery. Maximum recovery can be attained from ordinary foods purchased at your local supermarket.

4. *Develop other interests besides bodybuilding*: Many bodybuilders are notorious for having one-track minds. They walk, think, talk, eat, and sleep bodybuilding. Developing other interests and hobbies of a nondemanding nature, such as woodworking, auto mechanics, music, reading, and collecting, allows many individuals a chance to free their minds of training. The importance of a peaceful mind cannot be overstated. A person consumed by training anxiety will end up emotionally drained. Take time to incorporate other meaningful activities into your life, and then your muscles, when you do train them, will be more responsive.

Overtraining and Muscle Cell Destruction

In the January 1985 issue of *American Health* Stephen Kiesling writes:

> Rest isn't just a matter of making yourself feel better, it's essential to the very cells of your body. When Michael Sherman, then a research associate at Ball State University, aimed an electron microscope at the leg-muscle cells of marathon runners, he saw "twisted cells, torn cells, and cells turned inside out." And that was the day-*before*-the-race damage from training. The day *after* the event, even more cells were battered.
>
> In a related experiment, Sherman found that even after a full week of rest, marathon runners had not regained pre-race strength and power. Returning to moderate running after the marathon delayed recovery. And some races may take months to rebound from.

Few long-distance runners, however, heed Sherman's advice. Most continue to pound and mangle their bodies: step after step, day after day, week after week. Rarely do they take time to recover from the cumulative effects of such stress.

If marathon runners are the extreme in damaging their bodies as a result of overtraining, bodybuilders finish a close second with their multiple sets, giant cycles, and double-split routines.

Don't let yourself fall into the overtraining rut. Realize now that overtraining not only limits your results but also twists, tears, and destroys your muscle cells.

Above. A bodybuilder should always be prepared, says Mr. America Tim Belknap.
Middle. Scott Wilson enjoys a nutritious meal.
Below. Ali Malla shows Tom Platz his new bicycle.
Opposite. "To lift or not to lift?" that is the question. Sometimes your body is better off resting than training.

CHAPTER 3
SUPER HIGH-INTENSITY BODYBUILDING

A new training technique, called the 1¼ system, emphasizes the contracted position of certain exercises for super growth stimulation.

Chapter 3

Techniques: Understanding Super High-Intensity

"The barbell is certainly not perfect," says Arthur Jones, "but it's a damn good tool, a tool that is capable of producing outstanding muscular size and strength." That may sound strange coming from the man who invented Nautilus equipment, but it's true.

"The primary problem with a barbell," Jones continues, "is that it's misused. I seldom see a barbell being used correctly. Most bodybuilders require several years to get noticeable results, when, in fact, they could have received equal or better results in several months—if they had trained efficiently in proper form."

What are Jones's concepts of using a barbell efficiently in proper form?

Jones thoroughly detailed his concepts in two training manuals: *Bulletin No. 1* (1970) and *Bulletin No. 2* (1971). Both of these classic manuals were self-published and are no longer in print.

Fortunately, both bulletins were used in preparing my *High-Intensity Bodybuilding* book, which was published in November 1984. For the first time since the early 1970s, Jones's principles were applied to barbells and conventional equipment. The response to *High-Intensity Bodybuilding* was so great that this follow-up book on advanced techniques, *Super High-Intensity Bodybuilding,* proved necessary.

High-Intensity Guidelines

Before advanced techniques are described, it is important to review the basic high-intensity guidelines:

1. Perform no more than a total of twenty sets of all exercises in any one training session.
2. Train no more than three times a week. Each workout should involve the entire body, as opposed to splitting the routine into lower and upper body work on separate days.
3. Select resistance for each exercise that allows the performance of between eight and twelve repetitions. Higher repetitions, from fifteen to twenty, may be used for the lower body.
4. Continue each exercise until momentary muscular failure. When more than the guide number of repetitions are performed, increase the resistance by approximately 5 percent at the next workout.
5. Work your largest muscles first and your smallest muscles last.
6. Accentuate the negative or lowering portion of each repetition. Lift the weight in two seconds and lower it in four seconds.
7. Move slower, never faster, if in doubt about the speed of movement.
8. Attempt constantly to increase the number of repetitions or the amount of weight, or both. But do not sacrifice form in an attempt to increase the repetitions or weight.
9. Get ample rest after each training session. High-intensity exercise necessitates a recovery period of at least forty-eight hours. Muscles grow during rest, not during exercise.
10. Eat a balanced diet composed of several servings a day from the Basic Four Food Groups. Protein supplements and vitamin/mineral pills are not necessary.
11. Train with a partner who can reinforce proper form on each exercise.
12. Keep accurate records—date, order, resistance, and overall training time—of each workout.

For a complete understanding of these concepts, please read Part I of *High-Intensity Bodybuilding*.

Basic Routine for Advanced Bodybuilders

The primary difference between high-intensity training and super high-intensity training is the fact that the latter is harder. Any time your training becomes harder, it must also become briefer.

If you have been employing the high-intensity principles in your training, you'll need to modify only one guideline in applying advanced techniques to your workouts. You'll need to reduce the total number of exercises per training session by 20 percent. Thus, rule number one of the basic guidelines should be changed to read:

• *Perform no more than a total of sixteen sets of all exercises in any one training session.*

A tried-and-proved basic routine for advanced bodybuilders is as follows:

Exercise	Guideline for Repetitions
1. Leg extension with machine	12
2. Leg curl with machine	12
3. Donkey calf raise with partner	15
4. Full squat with barbell	20

Opposite. The rugged physique of Bertil Fox is a result of super high-intensity training.
Overleaf. Lee Haney is shown being helped with extra forced repetitions.

5. Straight-armed pullover with one dumbbell	12
6. Press behind neck with barbell	12
7. Behind neck chin-up with attached weight	12
8. Bench press with barbell	12
9. Bent-over row with barbell	12
10. Parallel dip with attached weight	12
11. Biceps curl with barbell	12
12. Triceps extension with one dumbbell	12
13. Upright row with barbell	12
14. Reverse curl with barbell	12
15. Stiff-legged deadlift with barbell	15
16. Trunk curl with weight behind neck	12

With some of the advanced routines, sixteen sets may prove to be too many. Remember, too much total exercise leads to overtraining and overtraining severely depletes your recovery ability. If in doubt about the total amount of training to do for maximum results, you are better off to undertrain than to overtrain. More will be said about this in the body-part chapters.

For now, let's examine closely the various advanced techniques that will be used throughout this book.

Regular or Normal

Regular or normal training is performed in the following manner. Lift the weight smoothly and slowly in strict style to the count of two. Lower the weight even more slowly to the count of four. Repeat the lifting, or positive phase, and the lowering, or negative phase, in that style until no lifting repetitions can be performed without cheating. This constitutes what is called momentary muscular failure, or more specifically positive muscular failure.

Training done in a regular or normal fashion is like a best friend. It is something you can frequently return to for dependable results. Furthermore, regular training done in a systematic manner provides you with a weekly or monthly method of charting your progress.

For example, let's say that during a workout in June you performed the press behind neck with 150 pounds for ten repetitions and failed positively on the eleventh repetition. Therefore, on your workout chart you recorded 150/10(R). The (R) denoted that the regular style of training was employed. Two months later, in August, you performed the same exercise for 180/10(R). Thus, with a few simple calculations, it is easy to determine that your press-behind-neck strength improved by 20 percent.

The amount of weight you can do for ten repetitions in a regular fashion is probably the easiest and most accurate way to measure your strength and chart your

Above. Perform each exercise until no further repetitions are possible.
Opposite, above. The barbell squat is still one of the very best bodybuilding exercises.
Opposite, below. Stiff-legged deadlifts should be emphasized on any basic routine.

...ybuilder, you should ...g approximately 25 ...der of your training...

...builder performing a ...uilders, in spite of ...too fast. Fast repe... individual muscle ...ortant in complete ...re, fast repetitions ...y from the muscles ...and connective tissues. Not only is this an unproductive way to build muscle, it is also dangerous.

One technique that I've used to convince bodybuilders of the importance of moving under control is called *super slow*. Super slow requires that you lift the weight in approximately ten seconds, then lower it to the beginning position in four seconds. Such a slow style of lifting was developed for use primarily with Nautilus equipment, but the principles can also be employed with some barbell exercises. The best barbell-dumbbell exercises to use in a super slow style are the ones that do not have sticking points during the range of movement. The bench press, squat, and curl all have sticking points, so they would not work as well as others. The barbell exercises that work the best are the upright row, lateral raise with dumbbells, calf raise, chin-up, dip, and the conventional leg extension and leg curl.

Since super slow is a demanding way to train, you must first reduce the normal resistance you would handle for ten repetitions by approximately 30 percent. Because of the slowness of your movements, you must also reduce the repetitions from eight to twelve to a range of four to six.

Breakdowns

One way to push a muscle past the point of momentary muscular failure is with breakdowns. When you perform the barbell curl with 100 pounds for ten repetitions and fail on the next repetition, you've failed because your strength has been depleted slightly below one hundred pounds—say ninety-five pounds. Ninety-five pounds of strength won't lift a one-hundred-pound barbell, so you fail. But if you had a magic wand that could instantly make this barbell lighter and lighter with each several repetitions, then you could effectively work past normal failure. And maybe working past normal failure would produce better muscle-building results.

With breakdowns, working past failure is possible. To do breakdowns, you'll need two training partners stationed at either end of the barbell to act as your magic wand. First, you must load each side of the barbell with a variety of loose plates and leave the collars off the bar. Then, when you reach normal failure, immediately your partners break down the weight by removing approximately 10 percent of the

Mark Marshall has the bar loaded to do breakdowns on the overhead press.

weight from the bar. This allows you to grind out another two or three repetitions. Finally, your training partners remove another 10 percent from the barbell, and you force out a final two or three complete movements.

Done properly, breakdowns may be just the stimulus you need to jolt certain muscles into growing.

Negative Training

Until 1972, few, if any, bodybuilders had ever tried heavy negative exercise. In the fall of that year, Arthur Jones wrote an article for *Iron Man* magazine that startled bodybuilders by challenging them to think not in terms of how much you can lift, but in terms of how much you can *lower*.

Jones found that most bodybuilders could lower under control 40 percent more weight with a barbell than they could lift. Lowering a heavier-than-normal weight has the potential to involve more muscle fibers and carry these muscle fibers to a deeper level of momentary muscular failure. For this book, two styles of negative training are recommended: negative forced and negative only.

With *negative-forced repetitions*, you perform a set of an exercise in the normal manner until positive failure. Then your training partner assists you in doing the lifting movement. Once the weight is in the top position, it's your job to lower it very slowly in about eight seconds. Your partner will help you once again to the top, and you'll lower in eight seconds. Three or four negative-forced repetitions added to the end of a normal set will soon make you appreciate the value of negative work.

The most intense form of negative training is *negative only*. You'll need two partners to do most of the lifting for you, which is a workout in itself. Start with a weight that is 40 percent heavier than you normally handle for ten repetitions. Your partners must do the lifting, and you do the lowering. It's important that you strongly resist the downward momentum of the barbell.

A properly performed set of negative-only exercise consists of three or four initial eight-second repetitions. The middle three or four repetitions are performed in six seconds. The last three or four repetitions are done as slowly as possible, which is actually faster than six seconds. You should discontinue the repetitions, despite your best efforts, when you can no longer control the lowering of the weight.

Negative-only work can be performed unassisted in two popular exercises: chin-ups and dips. You simply need to do the positive work with your legs, by stepping onto a chair to get into the top position, and then slowly lower your body with the strength of only your

---

Above. Jon Aranita performs inclined presses with dumbbells in a regular fashion.

Opposite. Juliette Bergman from Holland, winner of the Amateur Lightweight World Bodybuilding Championship in 1985, is 5'1" in height and weighs 114 pounds. Much of her dynamic physique is due to the fact that she always trains to failure and often extends the sets with negative-forced repetitions.

Bertil Fox knows the importance of finding a reliable training partner to assist him in all his exercises.

upper body. To make negative chin-ups and dips more intense, a weighted belt is attached to your waist.

Pre-Exhaustion

Pre-exhaustion is used to overcome one of the defects of most barbell exercises. In barbell exercises involving two or more muscle groups, failure is reached when the weakest group is no longer able to perform. In this case, little growth stimulation is provided for the stronger muscles involved in the same exercise.

In the bent-over row with a barbell for example, a point of failure is usually reached when the biceps of the upper arms fail. This normally happens before the larger and stronger latissimus dorsi muscles have been worked as hard as necessary to produce the best results. But by pre-exhausting the latissimus dorsi muscles the problem can be solved.

Pre-exhaustion of the latissimus dorsi muscles is done by performing a set of strict, stiff-armed pullovers with a barbell. Then instantly, with no rest, do bent-over rows. Now when you fail on the rows, you will fail from lack of strength in your latissimus muscles rather than from lack of strength in your biceps. With pre-exhaustion, your biceps are temporarily stronger than your latissimus dorsi and, as a result, your arms can be used to force your fatigued back to a deeper level of failure.

The recovery time of a pre-exhausted muscle is very brief, usually about three seconds. Thus, you must move instantly from one set of an exercise to the next set of another exercise with little rest in between—not even as much as four seconds. Four seconds or more will vastly reduce the growth stimulation.

Pre-exhaustion can be applied to almost any multiple-joint exercise. First, pick the muscle you want to pre-exhaust. Next, pre-exhaust that muscle by performing a single-joint isolation movement, and then instantly involve the same muscle in a multi-joint, compound exercise.

Other exercises that can be done in a pre-exhaustion style include leg extensions followed by squats, lateral raises followed by behind neck presses, biceps curls followed by chin-ups, triceps extensions followed by dips, and stiff-armed flies followed by bench presses.

When using pre-exhaustion, you will not be able to use as much weight in the follow-up multiple-joint exercise as you normally would, but you will stimulate far more muscle growth.

1¼ System

An advanced technique that has received almost no publicity is called the 1¼ system. Arthur Jones occasionally had Casey Viator use the technique to increase the intensity of some of his movements.

The contracted position of many single-joint exercises, such as the calf raise, shoulder shrug, lateral raise, leg extension, and leg curl, is the only position that involves the full length of the muscle. In many respects the contracted position is the most important because it involves the greatest amount of muscle. Yet

Canadian John Cardillo fights the negative portion of each repetition.

this important segment is often deemphasized by most bodybuilders. They frequently bounce in and out of the top position. Thus, the full value of the exercise is not realized and the resulting muscular development is incomplete.

For fuller muscular development you may want to try the 1¼ system in some of your sets. Here's what to do:

Reduce the weight that you normally do for ten repetitions by 20 percent. On the leg extension, for example, if you normally handle 150 pounds, reduce it to 120 pounds. Align yourself in the machine properly and smoothly lift the movement arm to the contracted position. Pause briefly for approximately one second. Lower slowly one-fourth of the way down and return smoothly back to the top position. Pause briefly once again. Lower back to the bottom. Repeat in the same fashion for eight to twelve repetitions.

After five or six repetitions, you will definitely start feeling a deep burn in your quadriceps. That's an indication that you're probably involving muscle fibers more thoroughly than you have in the past. And more thorough muscular involvement means better stimulation and more complete development.

Stage Repetitions

The newest advanced technique is called *stage repetitions* because the movements are done in parts or stages. Stage repetitions combine some of the best aspects of both super slow and 1¼ movements.

By combining these techniques, stage repetitions combat two of a barbell's primary limitations: the sticking point and the lock out.

The existence of a sticking point—the point during a barbell exercise when the resistance feels heavier than it does at other points—makes it obvious that your muscles are being worked harder in some positions than in others. Likewise, when you lock out your arms or legs under a barbell in certain positions, you should be aware that your muscles are not being worked. Your bones are supporting the weight and your muscles are merely acting as stabilizers.

Stage repetitions do not eliminate sticking points and lock outs, they allow you to work with and around them. Since a barbell curl has a sticking point, let's use it as an example.

The standing barbell curl is a single-joint movement that allows your hands to rotate approximately 150 degrees around the elbows. The sticking point, or the most demanding spot of the exercise, occurs when the forearms are parallel with the floor, or at a 90-degree angle with your upper arms. Here's how to make the barbell curl much more productive by applying stage repetitions.

1. Divide the range of movement into thirds.
2. Determine the hardest, next hardest, and easiest thirds, or stages, of the exercise.
3. Start with a weight that you can handle for twenty seconds in each stage, or sixty seconds for the entire set.
4. Perform the hardest stage first, the next hardest second, and the easiest last.
5. Raise and lower the barbell slowly throughout each phase for approximately eight to twelve partial repetitions.
6. Increase the resistance when you can do thirty seconds or more on each stage, or ninety seconds for the complete set.

In review, you work the middle 50 degrees of a barbell curl first and for approximately twenty seconds in a slow, controlled manner. Next, perform the top 50 degrees for twenty seconds. Finally, do the bottom 50 degrees for another twenty seconds. Performed properly, your biceps will ache clear to the bone.

Stage repetitions can also be applied to multiple-joint movements that involve lock outs. Once again you should work from the hardest stage to the easiest. The sticking point is the heart of the hardest stage and the lock out is at the end of the easiest stage. More will be said about stage repetitions in later chapters.

Effective and Efficient Action

One of the best things about advanced bodybuilding is that you can redesign your physique. You can concentrate on your thighs or specialize on weak calves. You can widen your back or define your waist. You can chisel your chest or peak your arms. And the most effective and efficient way to these goals is by using super high-intensity techniques and cycles.

The next eleven chapters will show you how to put these techniques into action. But in using any of the specialized cycles, maximum results will only occur if you adhere to the following rules:

- Perform the exercises exactly as described.
- Move quickly from one exercise to the next. Most of the advanced specialized cycles involve pre-exhaustion so they must be done with no rest between exercises.
- Repeat a specialized cycle no more than two or three times per week.
- Continue using a cycle for no more than four consecutive weeks. You may repeat the program again after three months.
- Combine your advanced cycle with other exercises for your overall body, but limit your routine to sixteen or fewer exercises.
- Do not perform more than two specialized cycles during the same workout.

It's now time to change into your training clothes and ready yourself for the most result-producing routines you'll ever experience. Let's move into action and force your muscles to start growing again!

Opposite, above. To perform negative-only squats, you'll need the help of two assistants to do the lifting at either end of the barbell.

Opposite, below. The hardest stage of the press behind neck is the middle one-third of the movement.

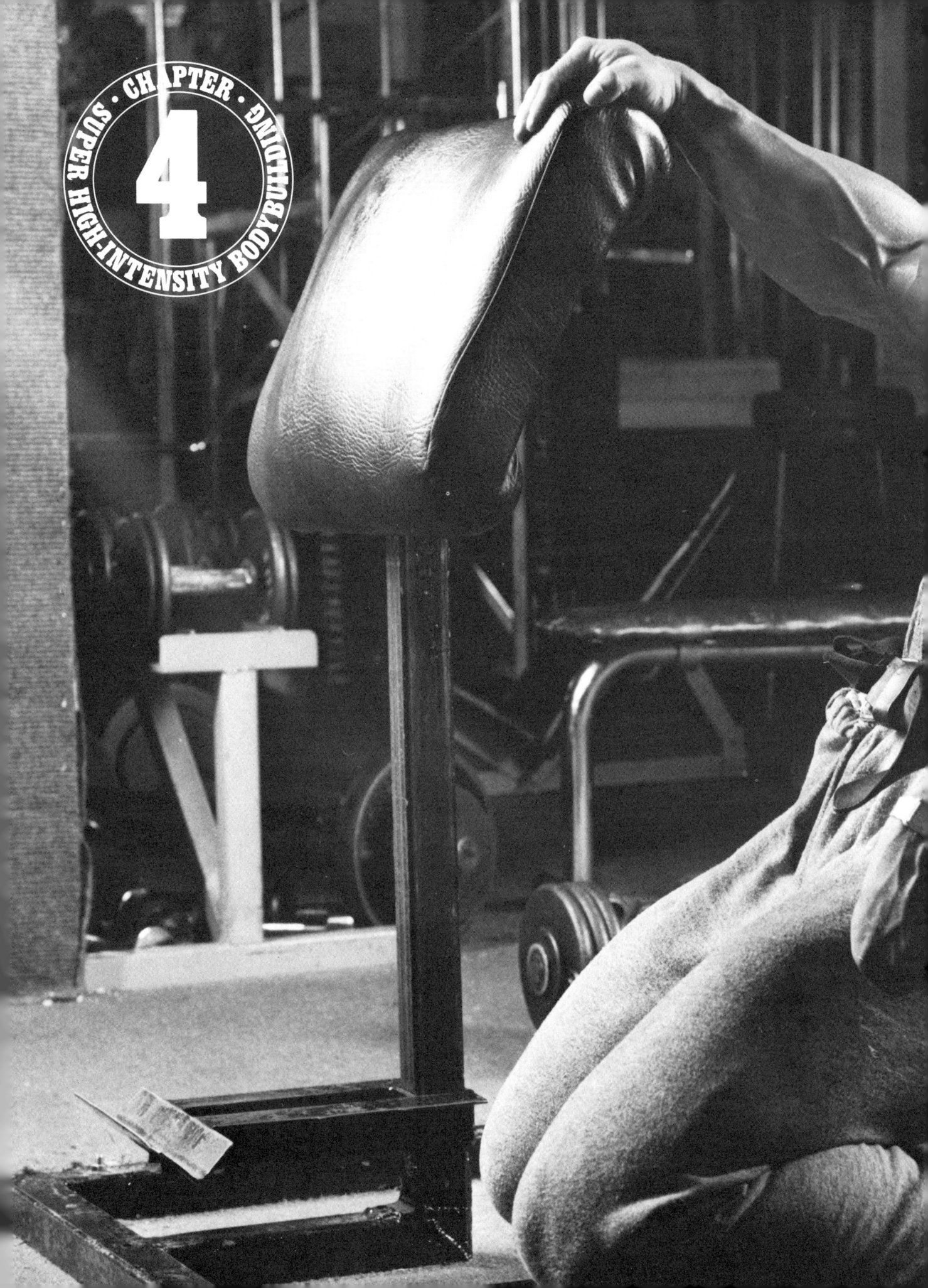

CHAPTER 4
SUPER HIGH-INTENSITY BODYBUILDING

The long-ignored sissy squat is one of the best exercises for your quadriceps.

Thighs:
Discovering an Old Method of Squatting

Bodybuilders can learn a great deal from the study of Greek mythology.

The legendary Hercules inspires us with his muscular size. Apollo makes a lasting impression on us with his symmetry. And Sisyphus teaches us about building massive thighs.

"Hey, wait a minute!" you say. "Sure, I know about Hercules and Apollo, but who's this guy Sisyphus?"

Sisyphus, as the legend goes, was the king of Corinth. He ruled with a harsh hand and soon became wealthy and greedy. The people he ruled eventually revolted, and the captured king was condemned to carrying a big stone up a steep mountain. When Sisyphus was almost to the top, invariably something would happen and the stone would come crashing down to the bottom. Sisyphus was doomed never to accomplish his mission, since the stone always rolled back down.

While Sisyphus was paying his debt to society, he was also building the finest pair of legs in ancient Corinth. The layback of his body as he angled up the mountain cradling the burden of a heavy weight no doubt caused his thighs to grow to gigantic size. Thanks to his massive legs and the indirect work he received on his upper body, Sisyphus could have probably become the first Mr. Greece.

Introducing the Sissy Squat

Thousands of years later in the 1950s, several California bodybuilders—with leg-development problems and a love of Greek mythology—saw in the Sisyphean torture a great muscle-building potential. They put two and two together, and that togetherness resulted in the modern, though often ignored, *sissy squat*.

I first heard about the sissy squat in 1960. Several articles in muscle magazines described this new technique and featured the outstanding legs of Steve Reeves, Doug Strohl, Reg Lewis, and Monty Wolford. I tried this unusual method of squatting, suffered through it, and gained over an inch on my thighs in less than three weeks. Believe me, the sissy squat is certainly not for sissies! It's one of the most demanding exercises you can do for your thighs.

The sissy squat more than any barbell or dumbbell exercise isolates your quadriceps by removing most of the involvement of the buttocks. Other squatting exercises involve rotation around the knees, hips, and lower back. The sissy squat concentrates on knee rotation only. This is accomplished by angling your body backward, rather than forward.

There are two ways of performing sissy squats: with weight and without weight. The routine below employs both styles in a unique pre-exhaustion cycle.

Sissy Squat Thigh Circle

The thigh cycle should be done exactly as described:

1. Leg extension, 1¼ system, immediately followed by
2. Leg curl, 1¼ system, immediately followed by
3. Sissy squat with dumbbells, immediately followed by
4. Sissy squat with bodyweight

Leg extension, 1¼ system: The 1¼ system requires that you do a quarter repetition immediately after the contracted position of each repetition. Sit in the leg extension machine and place your feet behind the roller pads. If possible, align the axis of rotation of the machine with your knees. Lean back and stabilize your body by grasping the sides of the machine. Straighten your legs smoothly. Pause at the point of full muscular contraction. Lower one-quarter of the way down, then move smoothly back to the straight-legged position. Lower to the bottom and repeat the 1¼ system for eight to twelve times or until momentary muscular failure. Instantly move to the leg curl.

Leg curl, 1¼ system: Lie face down on the machine and place your heels under the roller pads. Make certain that your knees are in line with the axis of rotation of the machine. Bend your knees and try to touch your heels to your buttocks. In the fully contracted position, your buttocks should be raised, and you should come to a complete stop. Lower the weight one-quarter of the way down and return it to the contracted position. Lower slowly to the bottom. Repeat each 1¼ repetition eight to twelve times.

Both the 1¼ leg extensions and leg curls emphasize the contracted positions of the involved muscles. The sissy squat places its emphasis on the stretched position of the quadriceps. Together they produce renewed growth stimulation.

The massive thighs of Roy Callendar.

Sissy squat with dumbbells: Have a long four-inch-high block upon which you can place your heels firmly. If you have a slippery gym floor, nail the block to a wide undersupport to prevent motion. In any case the block must not move and neither should your feet. Grasp a pair of light dumbbells with hanging arms. Arrange your heels upon the block so that they are almost shoulder-width apart. The dumbbells should now be hanging behind your buttocks. Your knees should be slightly bent and your body should be balanced.

Bend your knees slowly and lean your upper body backward at the same time. Descend as far as you can without losing your balance. Keep your hips thrust forward and your torso in line with your thighs. Raise your body by straightening your legs, but do not lock your knees. Keep them bent at the top. Begin the next repetition at once. Continue for eight to twelve non-stop, nonlock repetitions. Place the dumbbells on the floor and immediately do sissy squats with your bodyweight.

Sissy squat with bodyweight: Perform the identical exercise as above, using the same heel and hand placement, except without the dumbbells. Do at least twenty repetitions without weight, and at a slightly faster tempo. But do not increase the speed of the movement to the point where the depth of the squatting is decreased. Get a full, complete motion with each repetition. Halfway through the last set you should have one of the darnedest burns in your frontal thighs you've ever felt.

Thigh Specialization

I urge you to try this result-producing sissy squat cycle, but do not overdo it. Two or three cycles are not better than one. Remember, it's the intensity of the exercise that stimulates your muscles to grow, not the amount of exercise.

The frequency of such a pre-exhaustion cycle for your thighs should be no more than twice a week for four weeks in a row. And your overall workout should be limited to no more than sixteen exercises.

For example, your complete workout, which includes the sissy squat cycle, might resemble the following:

Thigh Cycle

1. Leg extension
2. Leg curl
3. Sissy squat with dumbbells
4. Sissy squat with bodyweight

Upper Body Exercises

5. Straight-armed pullover
6. Press behind neck

The barbell squat provides movement around the knees, hips, and lower back. The sissy squat places the emphasis on knee movement only.

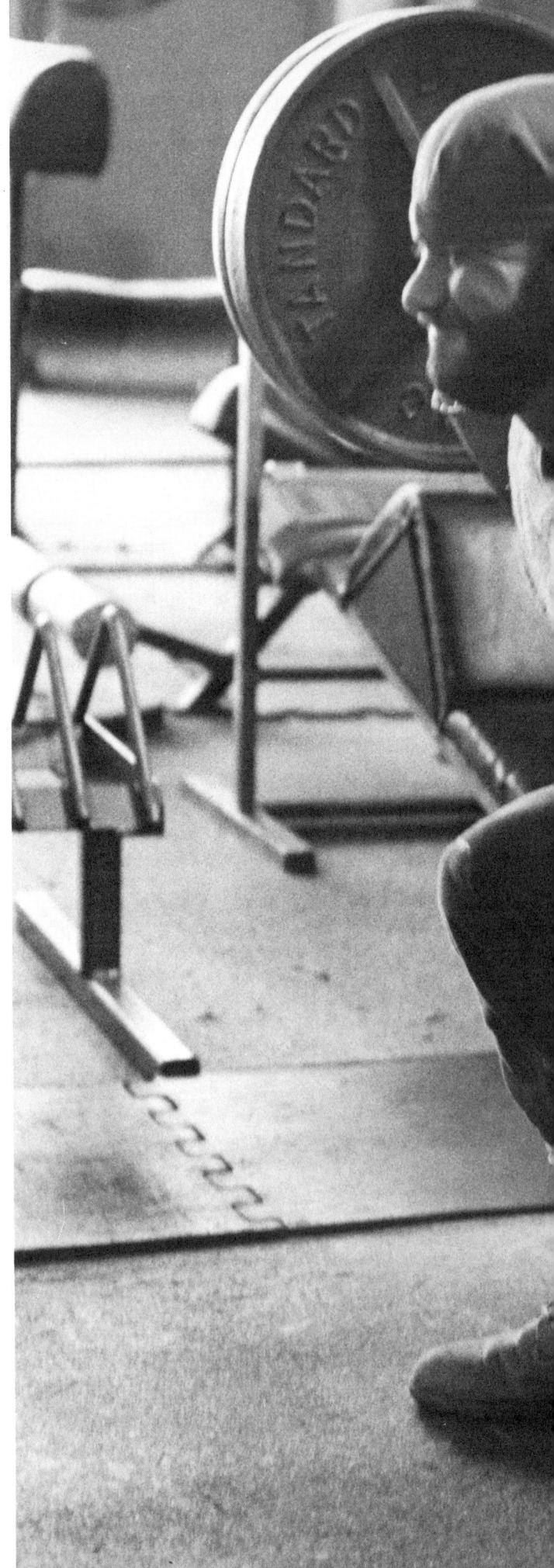

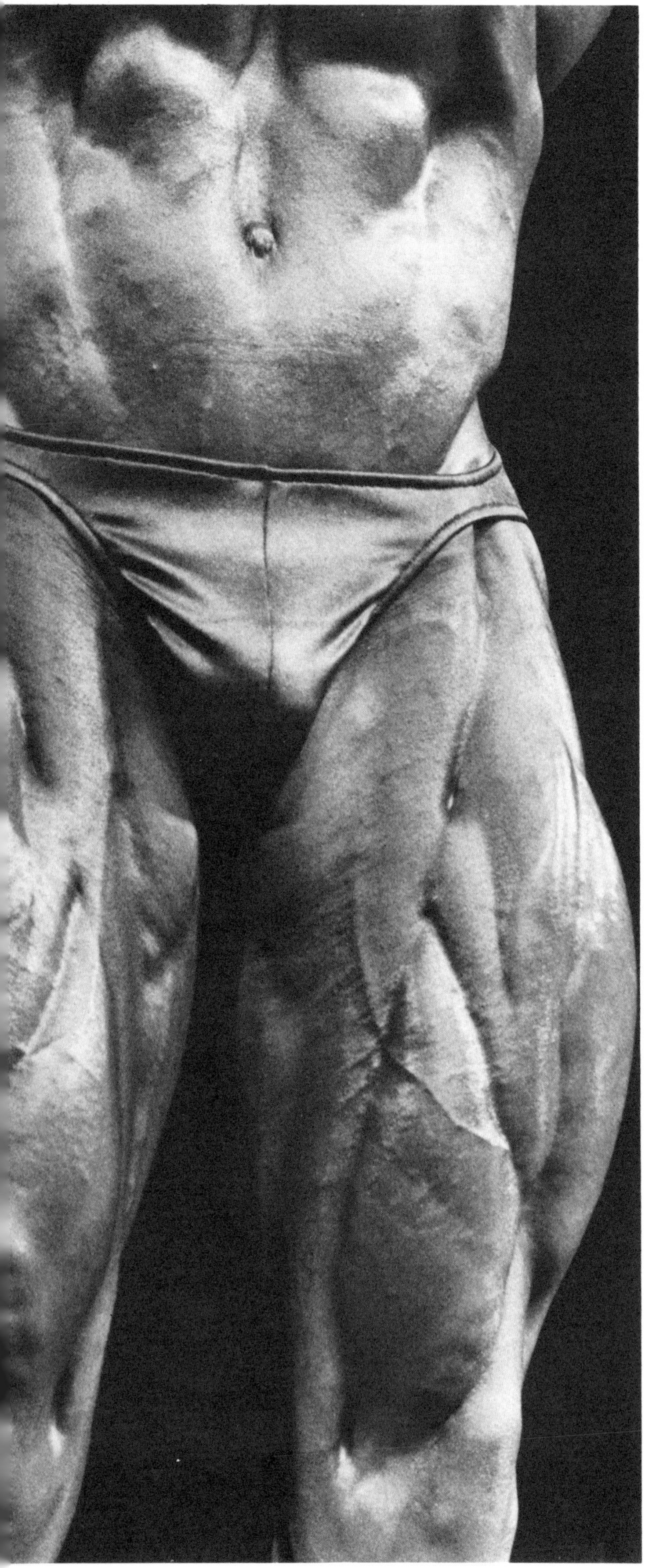

Chris Dickerson

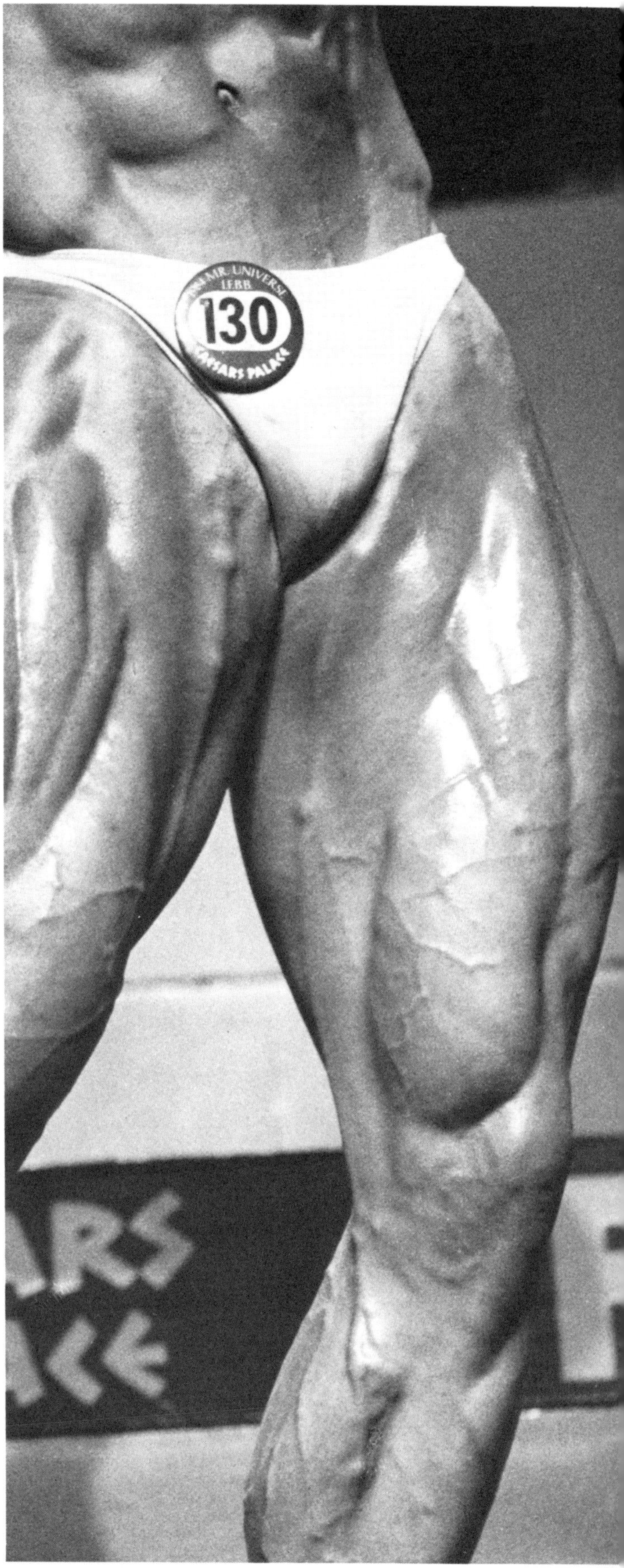

Berry DeMey

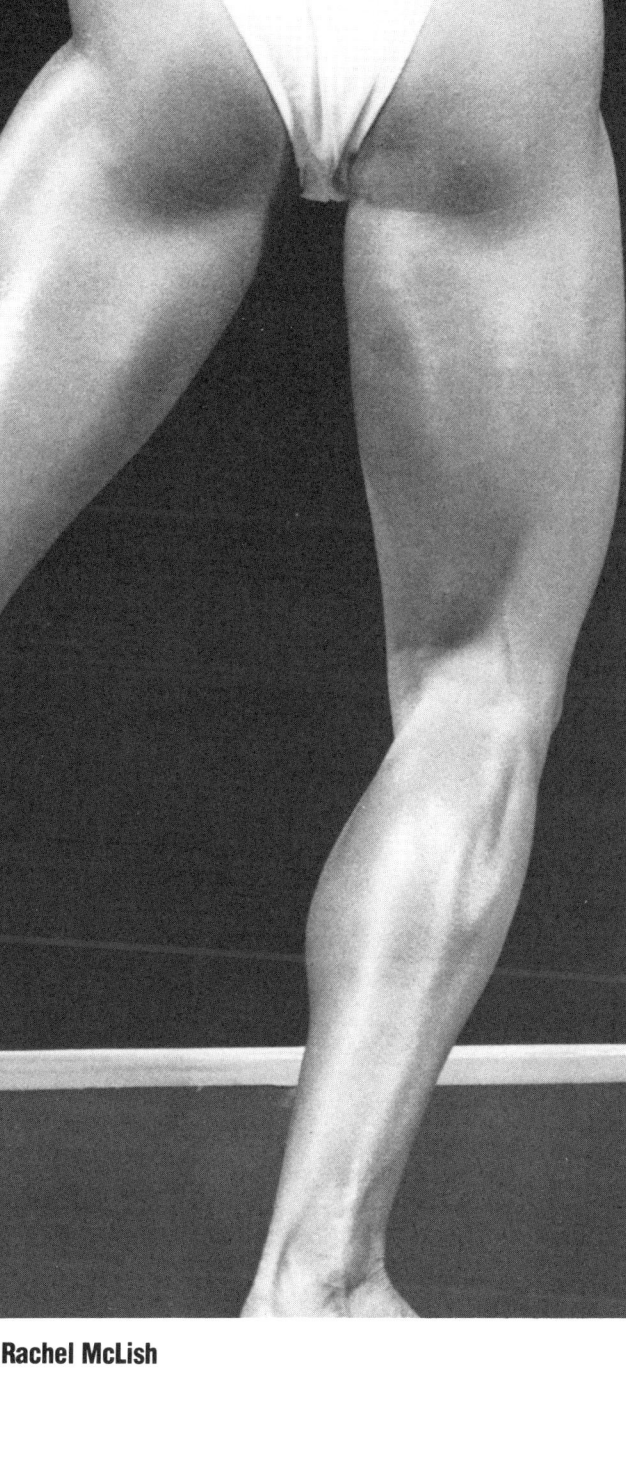

Rachel McLish

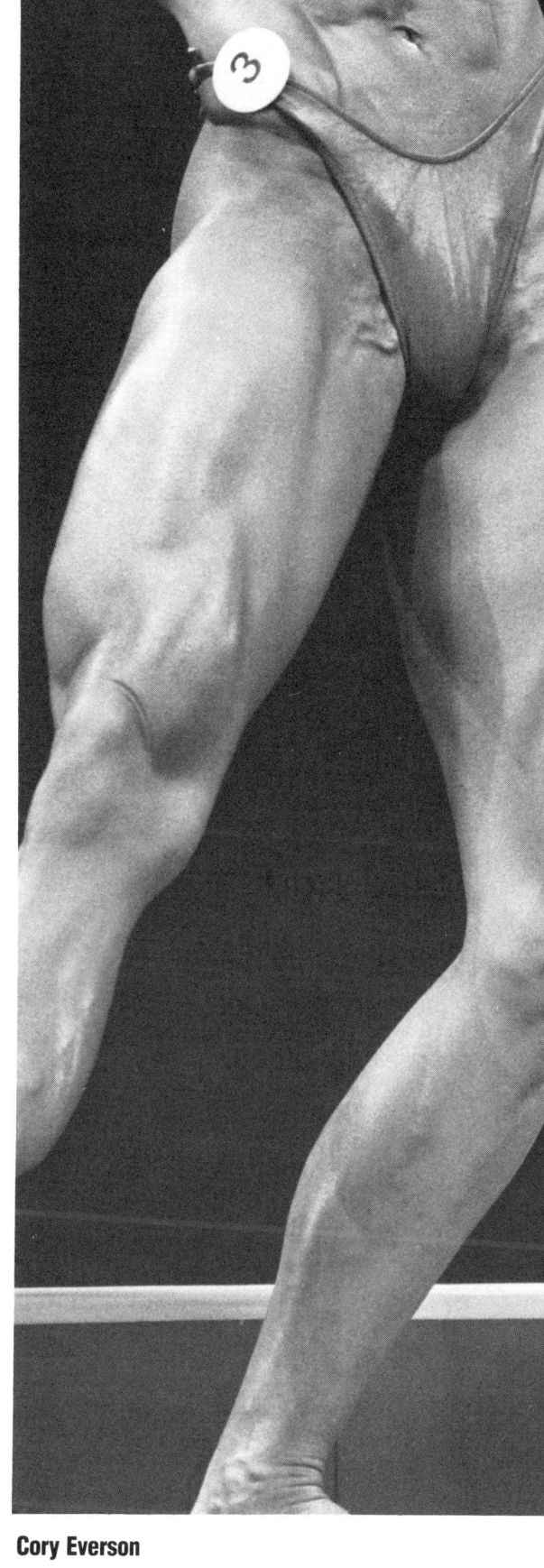

Cory Everson

Above. Leg extension, 1¼ system: Pause in the top position, lower one-quarter of the way down, and raise back to the fully contracted state.
Below. Leg curl, 1¼ system: The emphasis is on the contracted position of the hamstrings.
Opposite. Sissy squat with dumbbells: Lean back and bend only at your knees.

Sissy squat with bodyweight: Avoid locking your knees at the top and you'll get better results.

7. Behind neck chin-up
8. Bench press
9. Bent-over row
10. Parallel dip
11. Biceps curl
12. Triceps extension
13. Upright row
14. Reverse curl
15. Stiff-legged deadlift
16. Trunk curl

Exercises five through sixteen were taken from the basic routine section of the last chapter. An understanding of the guidelines in that chapter will provide you with valuable information on how to combine specialized cycles with overall-body routines for the most efficient growth.

Maximizing Results

From the above workout, it is important to remember that your body grows best by working it as an overall unit. If you want bigger thighs, you'll get them faster by working your upper body intensely as well. And the same concept holds true for specific upper body goals you may have.

Try to resist the temptation to perform more than two specialized, body-part cycles during the same workout. For example, you might employ either the sissy squat cycle and an arm cycle or the chest and forearm cycle on the same day. But once again, do not overdo specialization. Keep your body-part specialization brief and infrequent, and you'll be well pleased with the results.

The well-developed thighs of Samir Bannout, Tom Platz, and Casey Viator are the result of intensive leg work.

CHAPTER 5
SUPER HIGH-INTENSITY BODYBUILDING

Tim Belknap contracts his lower leg muscles.

Calves: Building Diamond-Shaped Lower Legs

Throughout my twenty-five years of being interested in bodybuilding, I've always admired shapely calves. As a result, I've always wanted to increase the muscluar size of my lower legs.

In 1963, during my freshman year at Baylor University, I was at the football stadium one day doing some sprinting on the grass. While alternating sprinting with walking up and down the field, I noticed two guys half way up the stadium stairs doing donkey calf raises. From fifty yards away I could tell that the bigger of the two guys had a terrific set of calves.

Eventually, I walked up and introduced myself to the fellows. The big guy with the outstanding calf development was Danny Ilse, a Mr. Texas winner from several years earlier. Danny had almost a perfect diamond shape on both the outsides and insides of his lower legs. And he had a deeply etched cut under each rounded lobe of his back calf when he contracted them.

What made Danny Ilse's calves even more spectacular was the smallness of his knees and ankles. They were almost delicate, which made his calves appear even more massive than they were.

The Donkey Calf Raise

Danny's favorite calf exercise, as you may already have guessed, was the donkey calf raise. Soon it would be my favorite too. In fact, the donkey calf raise is probably responsible for contributing more to lower-leg development than any other calf exercise in existence.

Donkey calf raises are effective primarily because of your body's positioning:

1. The bent-over position applies your partner's bodyweight in more of a direct line over your calves than would a barbell placed on your shoulders.
2. The bent-over position isolates the gastrocnemius muscles better by allowing you to keep your knees firmly locked. Bending the knees even slightly transfers some of the resistance away from your calves to your thighs.
3. The bent-over position allows more complete muscular contraction because you can get up on your toes better in the top position.
4. The bent-over position provides for more effective muscular stretch in that you can force your heels lower and lower in a progressive manner.

Thus, bodybuilders who desire the ultimate in calf development should make the donkey calf raise a featured exercise in their lower body routine.

Advanced Calf Cycle

All the exercises in the advanced calf cycle are performed back-to-back with no rest in between.

Belknap has some of the best legs in bodybuilding.

The diamond-shaped calves of Scott Wilson.

1. Calf raise machine, standing, immediately followed by
2. Donkey calf raise, immediately followed by
3. Donkey calf raise, stage repetitions

Calf raise machine, standing: You'll need a calf raise machine for this movement, or you may perform the exercise with a barbell that has been incorporated into a power rack. A sturdy four-inch block or step is necessary for standing on to allow for a full range of movement.

Place the balls of your feet on the block or step. Raise your heels as high as possible. Attempt to go higher by standing on your big toes. Lower your heels slowly to the stretched position. Try to go lower by curling and spreading your toes. Repeat the movement for twelve to fifteen repetitions. Move without resting to the donkey calf raise.

Donkey calf raise: Besides the sturdy block to stand on, you'll also need a chair to lean against and a training partner to straddle your hips. Keep your knees locked as you adhere to the four-part protocol that was described in the standing calf raise: (1) raise your heels, (2) up on your big toes, (3) lower slowly, and (4) curl and spread your toes. Repeat for twelve to fifteen repetitions or until momentary muscular failure.

At this point, there's a little trick that you must do before going into the next exercise. Bend your knees and allow your partner to jump off your back. Quickly stand up and raise your right foot and shake it for two seconds. Do the same thing for your left foot. The entire pause-shake should take no more than six seconds. Now assume the bent-over position and get your partner back in place on your hips.

Donkey calf raise, stage repetitions: Divide the calf raise into equal stages: top, middle, and bottom. Perform twenty seconds in the top one-third position. Do them slowly and try to get up on your big toes. Lower to the middle one-third and get another twenty seconds' worth. Now hit the bottom, stretched position for a final twenty seconds.

Go for the Burn

Fire! That's what your calves will be feeling from this cycle. That burn, however, will be quickly dissipated by blood being pumped in massive quantities to your lower legs.

Within three minutes after the termination of this routine, your calves should be pumped more than one inch larger than your normal measurements. And that means growth.

Calf raise, standing: Try to stand on your big toes in the top position.
Opposite. **Donkey calf raise, stage repetitions:** Since the top one-third of the calf raise is the hardest, perform it first for twenty seconds.

CHAPTER 6
SUPER HIGH-INTENSITY BODYBUILDING

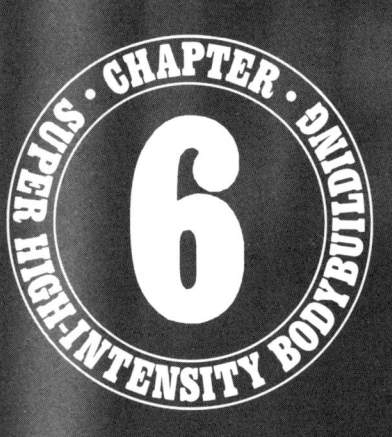

Grizzly Brown, a 320-pound wrestler-strongman from California, is known for his wide, thick back.

CHAPTER 6 · SUPER HIGH-INTENSITY BODYBUILDING ·

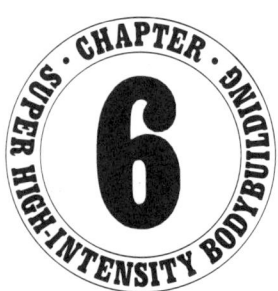

Back: Creating Thickness in Your Lats

A problem exists in trying to work your latissimus dorsi muscles, or lats, with a barbell. A barbell does not provide direct resistance for your lats. For the resistance to be direct, the force must be applied to the actual body part that is attached to and directly moved by the contraction of the muscles you're trying to work.

The function of your lats is to move your *upper arms* from an overhead position down and behind your torso. A barbell, unavoidably, must be held in your hands and your hands are connected to your forearms, not your upper arms.

Chinning-type exercises and rowing movements, for instance, are usually performed to work the lats. But these exercises also involve the bending muscles of the arms, the biceps. As a consequence, the relatively low strength of the biceps muscles results in poor exercise for your lats. Your exhausted arms force you to stop the exercise before your back muscles have been worked properly.

To work the lats correctly, the resistance must be applied directly against the upper arms. What happens to the forearms and hands during the exercise is not important as long as they don't get in the way of the movement.

These concepts were foremost in the mind of Arthur Jones as he set out to design the original Nautilus pullover machine more than twenty years ago. Jones was successful. In the Nautilus pullover, the resistance is applied directly against your upper arms or elbows. Your hands and forearms are not involved and remain relaxed throughout the movement.

The Nautilus pullover machine is a valuable tool in the

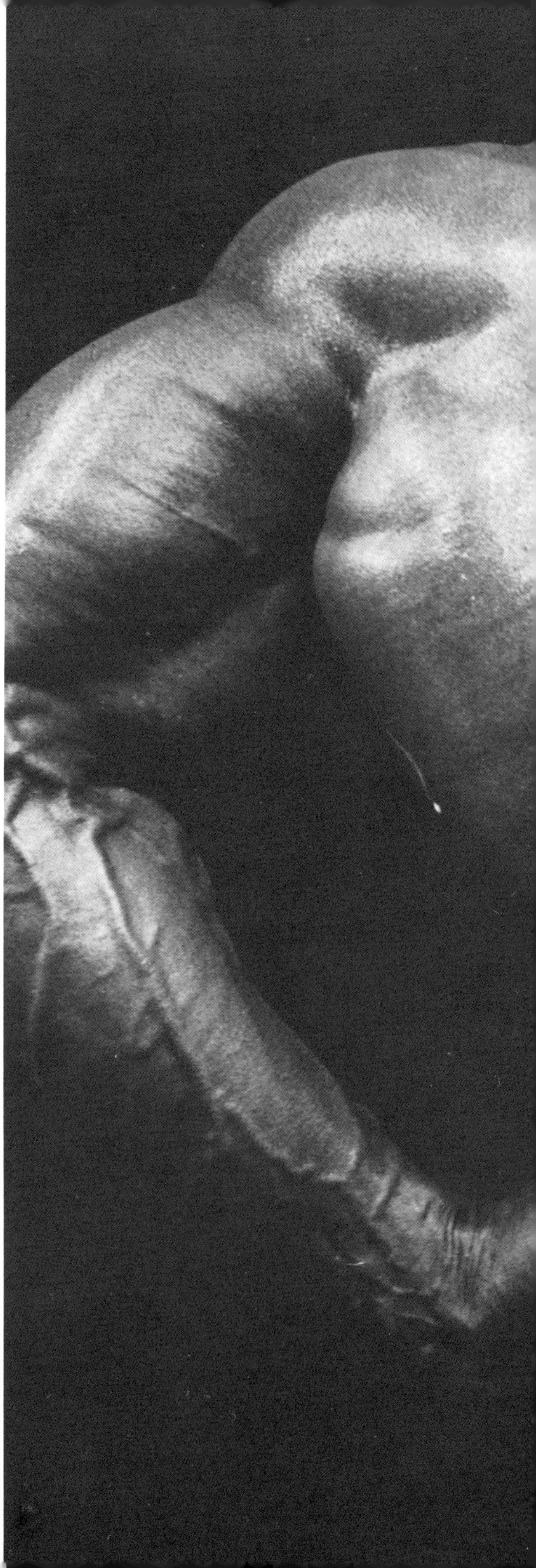

The tapered lats of Tony Pearson.

***Overleaf, left.* Mark Marshall spreads his wide lats.**

***Overleaf, right.* A back view of Cory Everson at the 1984 Ms. Olympia contest.**

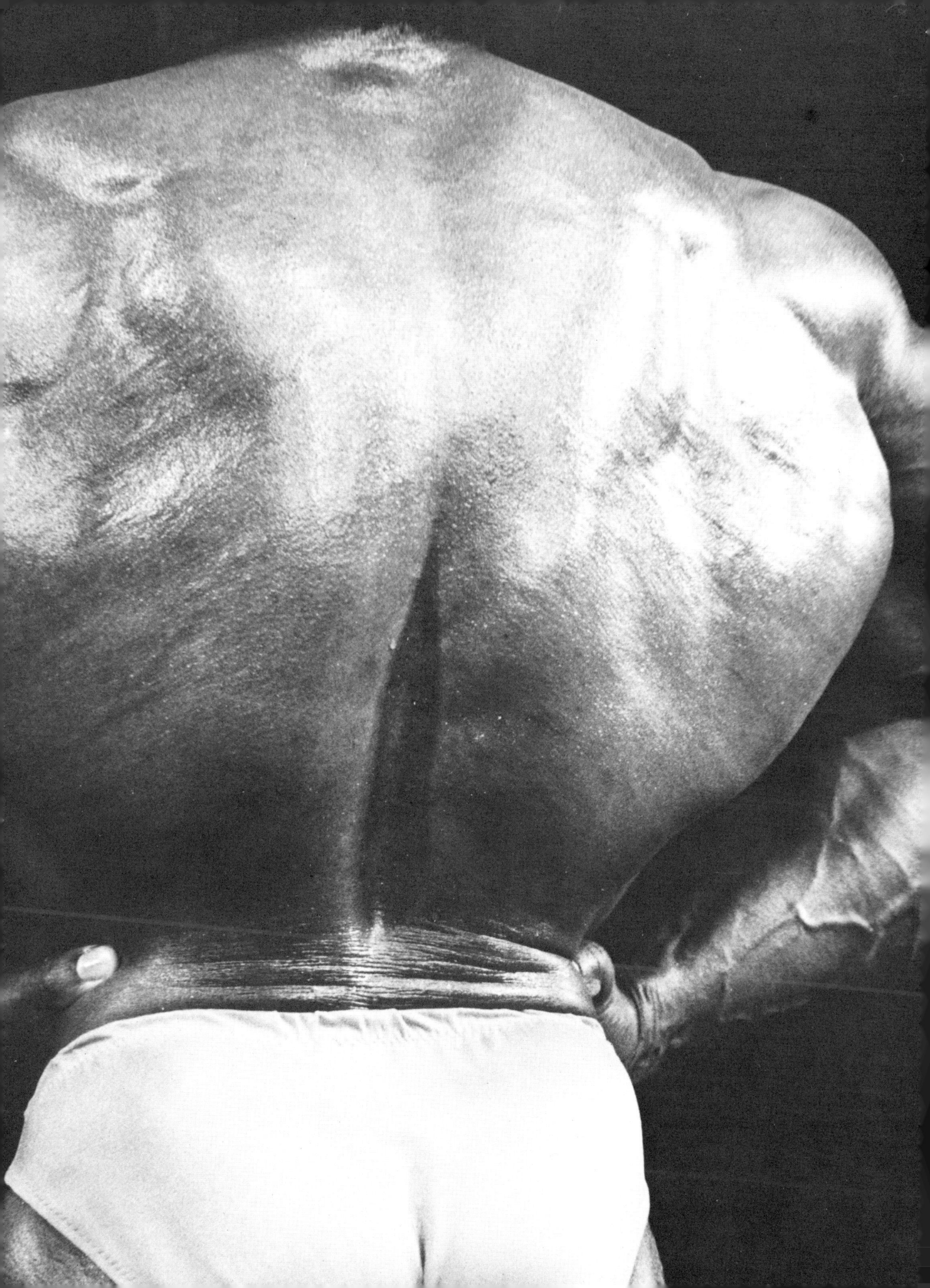

Above. Bent-over row, stage repetitions: Do not neglect the middle phase of the movement. Pull the barbell smoothly and slowly.
Below. Nautilus pullover, negative only: Notice that the resistance is on Bill Grant's elbows, not his hands.
Opposite. Behind neck chin-up 1¼ system: This exercise is a real killer. You may have to perform some of the repetitions in a negative-only manner.

development of wide, thick lats. Since it is found in most bodybuilding gyms across the country, it is included in the lat cycle. Bodybuilders who do not have access to the Nautilus pullover machine should substitute the bent-armed pullover with a barbell for it.

Advanced Lat Cycle

The advanced lat cycle may seem, at first glance, to be too brief. But after you've tried it, you'll know that this is not the case. The brevity of the cycle is necessary because of the super intensity inherent in each exercise. The cycle is as follows:

1. Bent-over row, stage repetitions, immediately followed by
2. Nautilus pullover, negative only, immediately followed by
3. Behind neck chin-up, 1¼ system

Bent-over row, stage repetitions: To prepare for stage repetitions, you must divide the bent-over row into three parts. The top one-third is the hardest, the middle is the next hardest, and the bottom one-third is the easiest.

Bend over and grasp the barbell using a narrow underhand grip. Your hands should be approximately four inches apart. Pull the barbell to your navel. Slowly lower the weight one third of the way down and smoothly return it to your midsection. Repeat the one-third lowering and raising for twenty seconds. Be sure to breathe continuously throughout this and other stages. Do not hold your breath.

Lower the barbell two-thirds the way down and smoothly raise it to the one-third level. Repeat the middle stage slowly for another twenty seconds. By now your involved muscles should be very fatigued, but resist quitting. Move into the last stage.

Slowly lower the weight to the bottom for a full stretch. Pause. Raise it back one-third of the way up. Repeat the lowering and raising for twenty more seconds. Place the barbell on the floor and swiftly move to the Nautilus pullover machine.

Nautilus pullover, negative only: No exercise bombards your lats as thoroughly as negative-only pullovers. Load the machine with approximately 40 percent more resistance than you normally handle for ten repetitions. You'll need one or two assistants to help you in doing the positive phase of the pullover. It is important that your assistants make the transfer smoothly to your elbows in the contracted position.

Pause with the movement arm on your midsection and rotate your upper arms slowly to the stretched position. The slow arm rotation should take at least eight seconds. On your verbal cue, the helpers should grasp the movement arm and bring it down to the contracted position. Repeat the slow lowering for eight to twelve repetitions.

By now your lats should be aching, but your biceps should be recovered from the first exercise. And you'll need all the biceps strength you can muster to perform

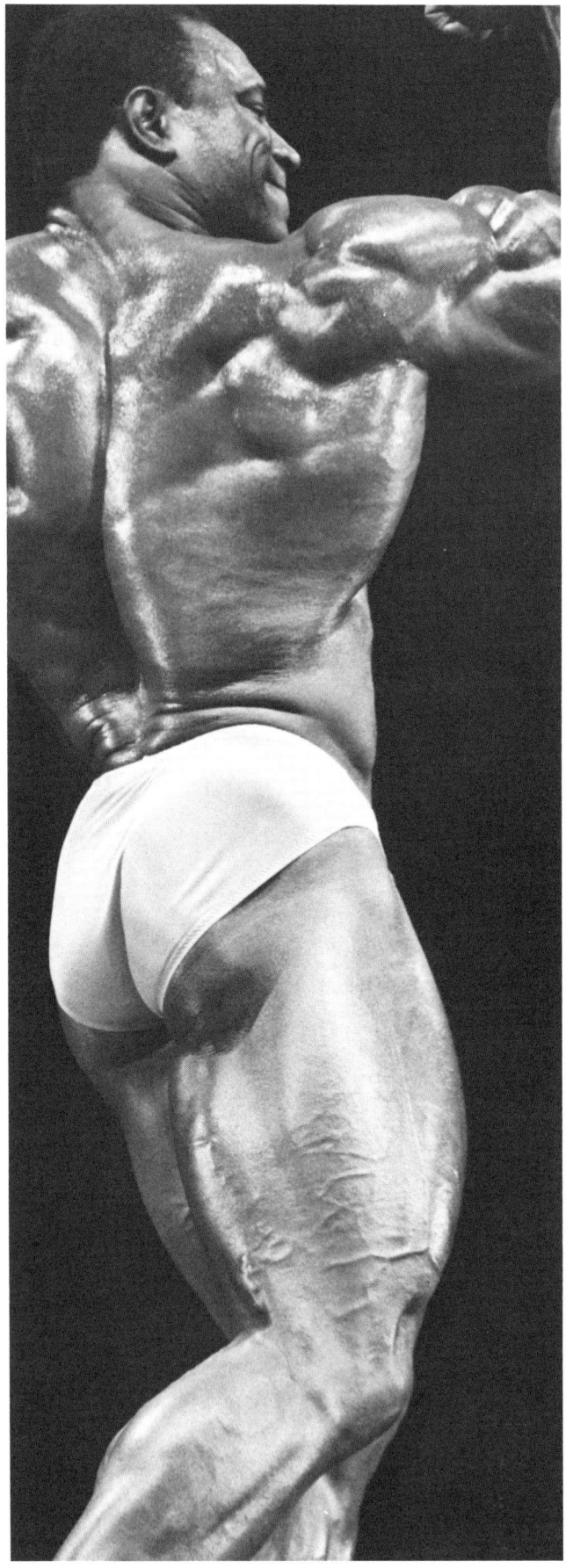

Lee Haney

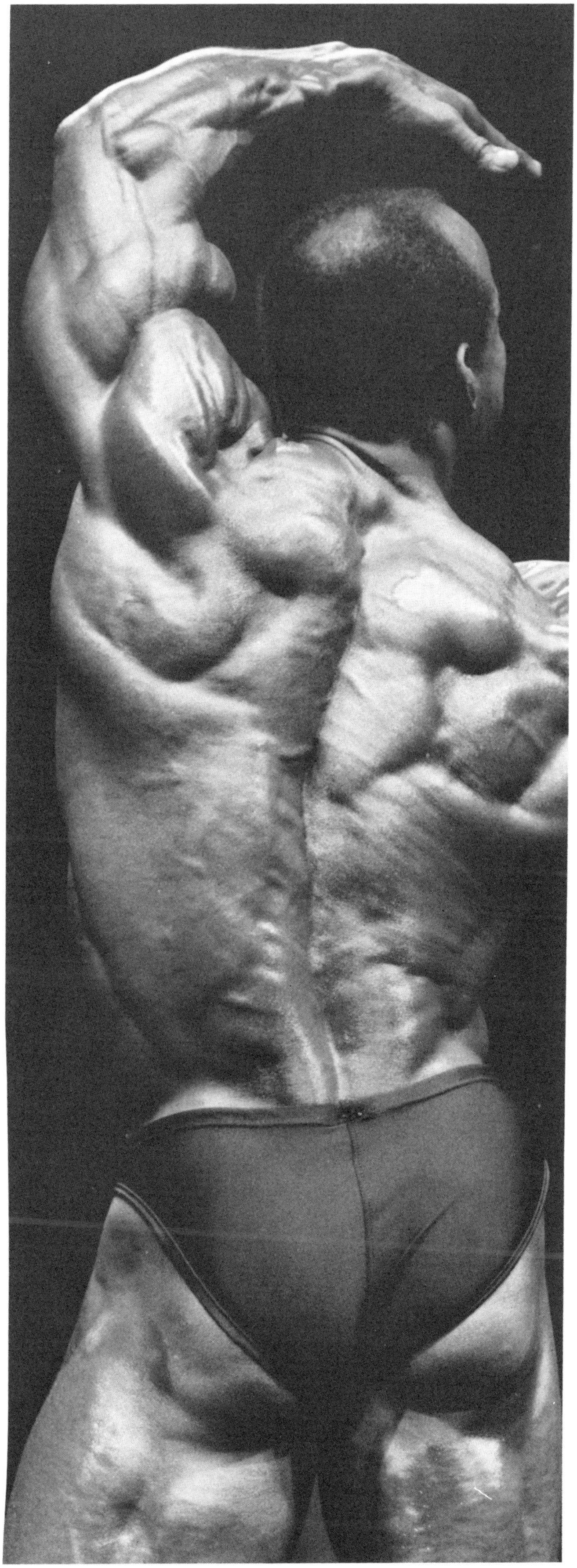

Albert Beckles

Clare Furr

83

chin-ups. The chin-ups will be used to force your lats to a deeper level of growth stimulation.

Behind neck chin-up, 1¼ system: Hang from a horizontal bar with each hand approximately six inches wider than each shoulder. Use an overhand grip. Pull your body up and forward until the bar touches behind your neck. Pause and lower one-quarter of the way down and pull back to the top position. Pause and lower slowly to the bottom. Repeat—if possible—for eight to twelve repetitions. "If possible" is used because most bodybuilders will be lucky to grind out four good repetitions using the 1¼ system.

If that is the situation you can do one of two things: (1) Have a training partner stand behind you and grasp your feet in a wheel-barrow manner and lift up on your legs as you pull with your arms. This will allow you to do several more repetitions. (2) Substitute the pulldown behind neck on a lat machine for the chin-up. You can simply perform the pulldown using the same 1¼ system for eight to twelve repetitions.

Combining the Lat Cycle with Other Exercises

After the advanced lat cycle, your lats should be thoroughly pumped. That's an indication that you're stimulating growth in many previously unused fibers. But to make sure your stimulated lats will grow, you've got to adhere to the basic high-intensity guidelines.

In training other muscles, you must limit your total sets per workout to sixteen or fewer. Subtracting the three exercises in the lat cycle from sixteen leaves thirteen remaining exercises or sets for your other body parts.

The following listing is another example of how a specialized cycle can be combined with other exercises.

Lower Body Exercises

1. Full squat
2. Leg curl
3. Leg extension
4. One-legged calf raise

Lat Cycle

5. Bent-over row, stage repetitions
6. Nautilus pullover, negative only
7. Behind neck chin-up, 1¼ system

Other Upper Body Exercises

8. Bench press
9. Shoulder shrug
10. Parallel dip
11. Lateral raise
12. Upright row
13. Triceps extension
14. Biceps curl
15. Side bend
16. Reverse trunk curl

A program such as this, which includes lat specialization, should continue twice a week for three or four weeks but not more than a month. After a month of the lat cycle, you may want to specialize on another body part, or you may go back to your basic routine. You may choose to concentrate on your lats again in three months.

Tina Plakinger, Rachel McLish, and Carla Dunlap compare backs during the contest which was featured in the movie *Pumping Iron II*.

Scott Wilson does seated overhead presses on a Nautilus leverage machine.

CHAPTER 7 · SUPER HIGH-INTENSITY BODYBUILDING

CHAPTER 7 · SUPER HIGH-INTENSITY BODYBUILDING

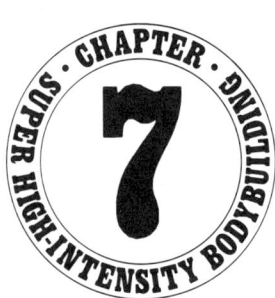

Shoulders: Widening the Triangle

All bodybuilders desire broader, more muscular shoulders. They want to widen the top of the triangle. A downward-pointing triangle is the image that forms in your mind when you draw a line from shoulder to shoulder and then connect the ends of the lines at your lower waist.

The shoulders and waist are natural focal points when the human body is viewed from the front or back. The width and narrowness of these focal points help to create an illusion.

Thus, if you want the broadest-possible-appearing upper body, you must not only develop your shoulders or deltoids but at the same time slim and muscularize your waist. Broad shoulders actually look wider when your waist becomes leaner. And your waist automatically appears smaller when your shoulders become wider.

Developing a lean waistline is the subject of a later chapter. This chapter, however, is concerned with building massive deltoids. The secret, once again, is high-intensity exercise.

High-Intensity Shoulder Cycle

The advanced shoulder cycle consists of three exercises performed back-to-back with no rest:

1. Lateral raise with dumbbells, stage repetitions, immediately followed by
2. Upright row with barbell, immediately followed by
3. Press behind neck with barbell, stage repetitions

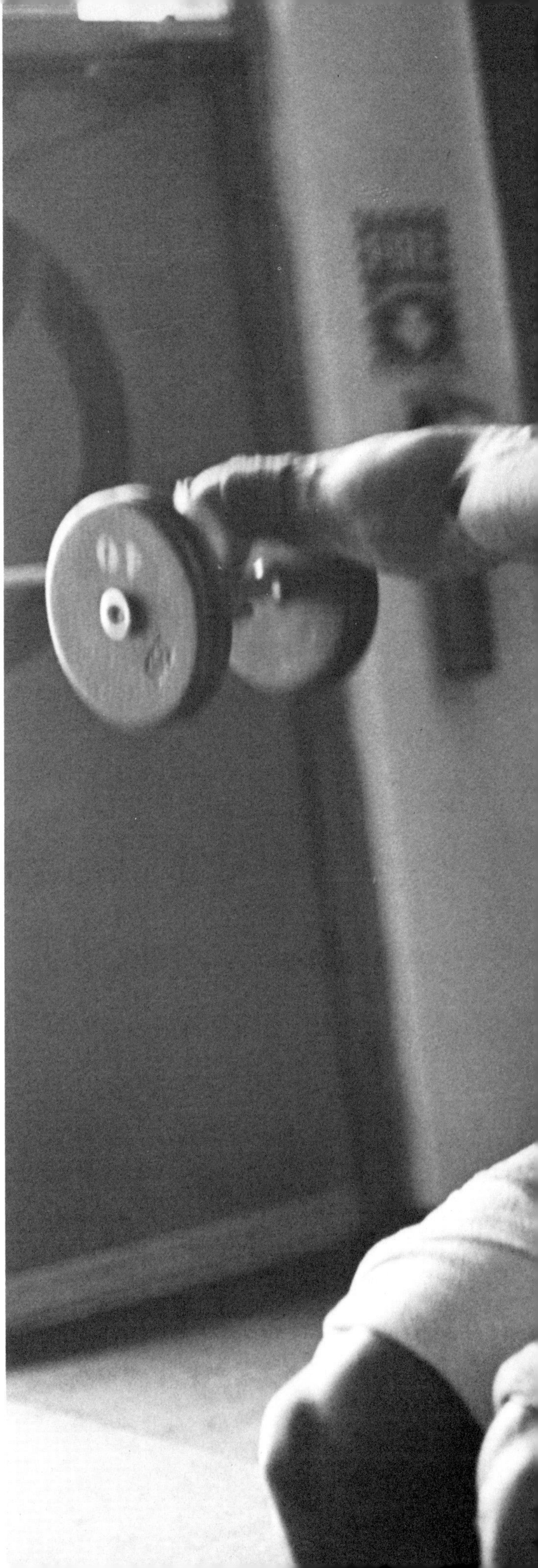

Lateral raise with dumbbells, stage repetitions: Emphasize the top position first since it's the hardest. Be sure to keep your elbows locked throughout the movement.

Overleaf, left. **Bob Paris is famous for his broad shoulders and narrow waist.**

Overleaf, right. **Gladys Portugues displays perfectly developed deltoids.**

Bertil Fox does presses with both barbells and dumbbells for complete shoulder development.

Tim Belknap often performs one-armed presses.
Opposite. Check out the rugged shoulders of Jim Hellwig.

Lateral raise with dumbbells, stage repetitions: Divide the lateral raise into three parts. The top part is the hardest because you are moving the dumbbells straight up. Do it first. The midrange is next, and the bottom one-third is last. The lateral raise may be performed seated or standing.

With the dumbbells in your hands, raise your arms sideways until they are slightly above the horizontal. Pause in the top position. Make sure your palms are facing down and your elbows are locked. Lower the dumbbells slowly one third of the way down and smoothly return to above horizontal. Continue the lowering and raising for twenty seconds.

Keeping your elbows locked, lower the dumbbells two thirds of the way down and smoothly return to the one-third level. Repeat the negative and positive segments for another twenty seconds.

The final twenty seconds is done in the bottom phase. Ideally you should continue lifting and lowering until you can no longer raise the dumbbells from your sides. Move quickly to the upright row.

Upright row with a barbell: The upright row brings into action your biceps and trapezius to force your pre-exhausted deltoids to a deeper level of fatigue. This barbell movement is performed in a normal, positive-negative fashion: two seconds up and four seconds down.

Grasp the barbell with a narrow overhanded grip. Stand and then raise the weight smoothly to your neck. Pause. Lower slowly to the bottom. Repeat for eight to twelve repetitions or until positive failure.

Place the barbell on the floor and go instantly to the press behind neck. Remember, the time between exercises in any pre-exhaustion cycle must be three seconds or less.

Press behind neck with barbell, stage repetitions: The hardest stage of the press behind neck is the middle one third, the next hardest is the bottom position, and the easiest is the top one third. In a standing position, place the barbell behind your neck. Your hands should be about six inches wider than your shoulders. *Note:* because of the intensity of this cycle, you will not need much weight for the overhead movement.

Press the barbell two thirds of the way up. Pause and lower one-third of the way down. Continue the pressing and lowering for approximately twenty seconds.

Lower the barbell to your shoulders and work the bottom one third of the movement for twenty seconds. Your deltoids should now feel as though they are about to burst. Don't worry, the last stage will ease some of the congestion.

Press the barbell to the fully locked out position. Lower one third of the way down and continue moving in the top one third for a final twenty seconds. To make the exercise harder, avoid locking your elbows until you simply can't stand the pain.

The Wide Illusion

That's it for shoulders! Three back-to-back exercises that must be experienced to be believed. After you've experienced the cycle, take off your shirt and stand in front of a large mirror. You'll soon see the effects of widening the triangle—and that's no illusion!

Grizzly Brown shows his style in the one-armed press. The dumbbell weighs 165 pounds.
Opposite. The award-winning shoulders of 1984 American Bodybuilding Champion, Mike Christian.

CHAPTER 8

SUPER HIGH-INTENSITY BODYBUILDING

Victor Richards bench presses a pair of 185-pound dumbbells.

CHAPTER 8 · SUPER HIGH-INTENSITY BODYBUILDING

Chest: Developing Powerful Pectorals

I entered my first bodybuilding contest in 1961, at age seventeen. The contest took place at the Southwest YMCA in Houston, Texas. I placed third. The thing I remember most, however, is not the contest itself but the teenager who had the best physique in the competition. His name was Ronnie Ray.

Ronnie was only slightly above five feet tall but he weighed a husky 170 pounds. I weighed about the same as Ronnie, except I stood a head taller and looked skinny in comparison to him.

The most impressive part of Ronnie Ray's physique was his chest. He had the most massive and powerful-looking pectoral muscles that I have ever seen on a teenager.

Three years later, Ronnie and I became good friends. He owned a business in Dallas, and I was attending Baylor University in Waco. We would frequently visit with each other at weightlifting and bodybuilding contests throughout Texas and Oklahoma.

In the 1960s, many competitors—at least those from Texas—would enter both the physique and the lifting contests. Powerlifting in those days consisted of the standard lifts: squat, bench press, and deadlift, and sometimes the curl and upright row. Ronnie and I usually entered both competitions.

Ray's specialty was the bench press. In fact, in the first powerlifting contest he entered, he bench-pressed more than he squatted or deadlifted. Several years later, however, that wasn't the case. Ronnie worked hard on the squat and deadlift and became a champion in both—and an overall National Champion in the 181-pound class. Plus, he established American and world records numerous times in the bench press, having done well over 500 pounds while weighing under 200 pounds.

Watching Ronnie train and compete was a meaningful experience. All of his training repetitions and maximum attempts were performed in the absolute strictest style. While most of his competitors would use any tactic they could get away with, such as bouncing the bar off their chest, short-ranging the squat, or hitching on a deadlift, Ray refused to compromise. He always exceeded the requirements of the rule book.

His bench presses were a work of art. I've seen him do 400 pounds for six strict repetitions—and he paused with the bar on his chest for a full ten seconds before each movement. Furthermore, many of his repetitions were done in a super slow style. Ray may have been the first person to experiment with very slow, controlled repetitions.

In my opinion, Ronnie's powerful pectorals and overall body strength were primarily a result of the excellent style of performance that he employed on all his exercises. If you want a massive chest, take a tip from Ronnie Ray and pay particular attention to *feeling the resistance* in each point throughout the range of movement in all your repetitions. This certainly makes the exercise harder, but it also makes it more productive.

Advanced Chest Cycle

The advanced chest cycle is brutally hard. It consists of the following four exercises:

1. Nautilus 10° chest machine, 1¼ system, immediately followed by
2. Bench press to neck, breakdowns, immediately followed by
3. Parallel dip, negative only, immediately followed by
4. Push-up on floor with bodyweight

Nautilus 10° chest machine, 1¼ system: Direct resistance for the pectoralis major muscles is provided by the Nautilus 10° chest machine. If this machine is not available, you may substitute the arm cross on the Nautilus double chest machine, or the bent-armed fly with dumbbells.

Lie on your back with your head higher than your hips. Place your arms under the roller pads. The pads should be in the crooks of your elbows. Move both arms in a rotary fashion, until the roller pads touch over your chest. Pause. Lower slowly one fourth the way down and move back to the contracted position. Lower slowly to the bottom. Repeat the entire system for eight to twelve repetitions. Move quickly to the bench press to neck.

Bench press to neck, breakdowns: You'll need about 30 or 40 percent less resistance on this exercise than you normally use in the bench press for ten repetitions. Also, you'll need to prepare the barbell for one breakdown by leaving the collars off and having some small plates for quick removal at each end. The breakdown should be approximately 20 percent of the weight on the bar, or 10 percent from each end.

Grasp the barbell slightly wider than the width of your shoulders and bring it to arm's length over your chest.

The massive, muscular chest of Lee Haney is shown to his advantage in this pose.

Clare Furr

Rachel McLish

Lower the barbell slowly, keeping your elbows wide, and lightly touch it to your neck. Press the weight smoothly to the top position and repeat it for eight to twelve repetitions.

On the last repetition pause in the top position and have two assistants remove 10 percent from each end of the barbell. Continue performing slow, smooth repetitions until positive muscular failure. Replace the bar on the racks and instantly move to the parallel bars.

Parallel dip, negative only: The 10° chest and the bench press should have thoroughly pre-exhausted your pectorals. The dip, performed in a negative-only manner, will require your triceps to force your pectorals to work even harder.

Place a chair or sturdy box between the dip bars. Climb to the top position. Straighten your arms, remove your feet from the chair, and stabilize your body. Lower slowly to the stretched position. This negative movement should take a full eight seconds. Climb back quickly to the top and repeat for eight to twelve slow repetitions. If you can perform more than twelve repetitions, you'll need to add extra resistance to your bodyweight. This can be in the form of a dumbbell to a waist belt.

Push-up on floor: You won't feel like doing push-ups after the dips; in fact, you may not be able to do even one—but give them a try. With your hands directly under your shoulders, do as many push-ups as you can in a normal fashion. Then, do several more in a negative manner by using your knees to assist you in getting into the locked-out position. Slowly lower your chest to the floor.

Maximizing the Chest Cycle

The chest cycle, performed correctly, should require approximately six minutes, but as a result of that six minutes, your chest should be engorged with blood—blood that will stimulate your pectoral muscles to grow larger and stronger. Remember, the key to building your pectorals is *strict style* and *feeling the resistance* throughout each repetition.

Do not try to specialize on your chest and shoulders during the same workout. There is too much transfer from one body part to the other. Ideally, you should limit the chest cycle to two workouts per week and to no more than one out of every three months.

Massive pectorals and awesome power can be yours with this super high-intensity chest cycle.

One of the most popular chest exercises is the inclined dumbbell fly.
Opposite. The imposing chest and upper body of Mike Christian.
Overleaf. Nautilus 10° chest machine, 1¼ system: Isolate your pectorals without involving your triceps.

Above. Inclined presses are demonstrated by Peter Paul.
Below. Push-up on floor: Finish off your chest by doing as many normal push-ups as possible.
Opposite. The superb pectorals of Roy Callendar.

CHAPTER 9
SUPER HIGH-INTENSITY BODYBUILDING

Tim Belknap is pictured in the middle of a set of cable curls.

Arms:
Concentrating on Your Biceps and Triceps

"I can add a quarter of an inch on my arms," Arthur Jones commented to me one day, "by just *thinking* about training my biceps and triceps."

Some people may believe Jones is kidding, but not me. I've seen him train his arms and he exerts more concentration during his repetitions than anyone I've ever observed. And Jones does his concentration with an expressionless face.

While most people resort to tortuous grimaces and moans during their repetitions, especially the last ones, Arthur remains calm and controlled. It almost looks as though he is not working to his capacity until afterward when you notice the pump and the muscle-building results he gets.

"When I really concentrate on doing a curl," Jones said, "muscular contractions begin occurring in my biceps—before overt movement is noted. Thus, after laying off training for several months, the mere thought of working my arms produces an overnight increase in their size."

What gives with Jones? Is he using mind over matter?

In a way he is. Exercise physiologists find that by placing an electromyograph on certain muscle groups and merely thinking about their contraction produces tiny signals of activity in those muscles. Faint contractile changes take place that rehearse the actual movement.

The relaxed upper body of Victor Richards looks impressive from all angles.
Overleaf, left. The horseshoe-shaped triceps of Robby Robinson.
Overleaf, right. The peaked biceps of Albert Beckles.

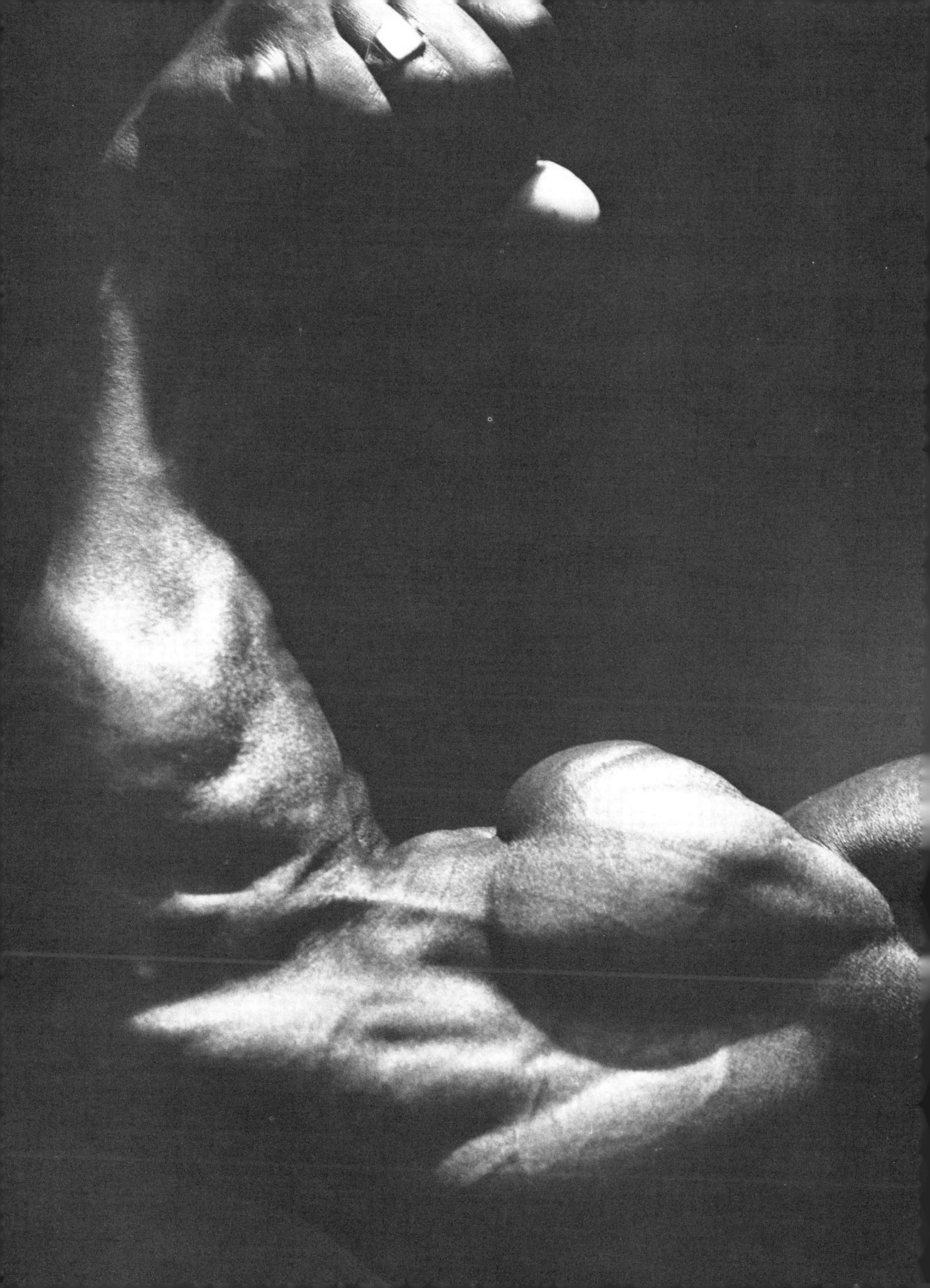

The simple test below will illustrate the importance of concentration in training.

The Pendulum Test

First cut a piece of string about ten inches long. Attach a small key to one end. Now take a piece of white unlined paper and draw on it a circle about two inches in diameter.

Read these instructions through first, then actually perform this test in quiet surroundings.

Sit at a table. Rest your left arm comfortably on the table. Place your right elbow on the table and hold the end of the string in your hand with your wrist slightly forward. Place the paper under the pendulum so that the center of the circle is directly below the key. Hold the string so the key just clears the paper. Loop the string over your first finger for stability. Now adjust your body so as to be very comfortable. If you are sitting properly, the pendulum should hang in front of the center of your body and the key should be about half an inch above the top of the table.

Remain at ease for a few seconds. The pendulum is motionless. Concentrate on the key and mentally visualize it beginning to move gently back and forth, left to right, right to left, left to right, right to left. Actually *will* it to move. The pendulum is swinging.

Put this book down on the table. Read the pendulum text over, stopping at each paragraph to carry out the instructions.

Once you have demonstrated that visualizing the key to move does result in movement, you can heighten this process by concentrating on the pendulum going in a circle. Now make it go around the other way by visualizing it to reverse itself.

You are not consciously exerting any effort to swing the pendulum. But by visualizing and thinking about the movement, you are influencing your subconscious to perform the necessary manipulation of your hand.

Mental Practice

It is commonly assumed that most of the bodybuilding process is physical. Although physical training is indispensable for acquiring a well-built body, mental practice is also important. Mental practice is seeing a definite performance in your imagination.

Arthur Jones used mental practice in "thinking about training" his biceps and triceps. That concentrated thinking, if it is strong and visual enough, can actually produce measurable stimulation and overcompensation in your arms and is certainly worth using.

The primary advantage of mental practice is that you can mentally perform your workouts using proper form and intensity, making repetition increases in all your exercises, 100 percent of the time. You'll never have a bad workout and you'll always accomplish your goals—given that you know how to accomplish your goals.

Advanced Arm Cycle

If larger and stronger arms are two of your goals,

Above. Samir Bannout and Grizzly Brown compare their arms.
Below. Barbell curl, stage repetitions: *Concentration* and *control* are the key concepts in performing this productive exercise.
Opposite. Concentration is one of the factors in Tom Platz's phenomenal development.
Overleaf. The flexed arms of Tim Belknap (left) and Ray Mentzer (right).

then this advanced arm cycle will help you accomplish them. Study the following exercises carefully. Concentrate on them beforehand and rehearse them mentally before performing the cycle.

1. Standing curl with barbell, stage repetitions, immediately followed by
2. Chin-up, super slow

Rest for one minute.

3. Triceps extension with one dumbbell held in both hands, stage repetitions, immediately followed by
4. Parallel dip, super slow

Standing curl with barbell, stage repetitions: Divide the curl into three stages: bottom, middle, and top. The middle is the hardest, the top is the next hardest, and the bottom is the easiest.

Grasp the barbell with an underhanded grip and stand erect. Curl the barbell smoothly two-thirds the way up. Lower one-third the way down. Continue working in the middle range of the movement for twenty seconds.

Curl the barbell to the top position while keeping your elbows in line with your torso. Do not let your elbows move forward. Lower the weight one third the way down from the top. Lift the barbell to the top position. Repeat for another twenty seconds.

The last twenty seconds is done in the bottom one-third stage. Lower the weight and raise it to the one-third level. Continue until positive failure. Move directly to the chin-up, which will require your utmost concentration.

Chin-up, super slow: The protocol for super-slow chin-ups is ten seconds for the pulling up and four seconds for the lowering.

From a hanging, underhanded position, start pulling up very slowly. Have a friend give you a ten-second count. At five seconds you should be half way up. Pause at the top and take four seconds to lower. Your initial goal in the chin-up should be only four repetitions, but these four repetitions will be more than many bodybuilders can perform.

If you cannot perform four repetitions, have your training partner hold your feet and assist you in getting to the top position. On the other hand, when you can do more than six super-slow repetitions, you'll need to add a small dumbbell to a waist belt and hang it from your hips.

Have a drink of water during your one-minute rest period and visualize your next two exercises: triceps extensions followed by dips.

Triceps extension with one dumbbell held in both hands, stage repetitions: Divide the triceps extension into thirds. The middle one-third is the hardest, the bottom one-third is the next hardest, and the top one-third is the easiest since it involves a lock out.

Grasp one dumbbell in both hands and press it over

Mr. Canada winner, Calvin Nyuli, forces one more repetition from his triceps.

Lee Haney performs one-armed triceps extensions.

your head. Your elbows should be close to your ears. Bend your arms and lower the dumbbell two thirds the way down. Lift and lower smoothly in the middle range for twenty seconds.

Lower to the stretched position and work in the bottom one-third stage for another twenty seconds. Be sure to keep your upper arms vertical and your elbows pressed tightly against your head.

Raise the dumbbell to the top and lower it one third the way down. Repeat the positive and negative stage for a final twenty seconds. Place the dumbbell on the floor and move immediately to the parallel bars.

Parallel dip, super slow: Begin in the stretched position, with your arms bent. Slowly, inch by inch, move your body up toward the locked out position. You should reach the top at the count of ten. Lower in four seconds and repeat the ten-second positive and four-second negative movements for four repetitions. Concentrate on each repetition and give it your all.

If you need help, have your partner assist by lifting your feet. Once the exercise becomes easy, add more resistance around your waist or hips.

Your Best Effort

Perform the arm cycle two or three times per week for no more than one month out of every three. Do the cycle toward the end of your overall workout, after you've worked your legs and torso. Keep accurate records of your resistance, repetitions, and seconds (time). And most of all, do not neglect the mental aspects of training your arms.

All four of the upper arm exercises will tax both your physical and mental faculties. By combining concentrated efforts in both areas, your arms will ache, pump, and grow to new heights.

Give the cycle your best effort.

Above. A low angle of Tim Belknap doing pulley triceps extensions.
Middle. Parallel dip, super slow: It is important to keep track of your raising and lowering time for each repetition.
Below. Bertil Fox pumps his arms with triceps pushdowns.
Opposite. Alternate dumbbell curls are a favorite with Tim Belknap.

CHAPTER 10
SUPER HIGH-INTENSITY BODYBUILDING

Wrist curls with a barbell are one of the best exercises for your forearms.

Chapter 10 — Super High-Intensity Bodybuilding

Forearms:
Getting a Grip on Massive Development

In October 1984, Jim Flanagan, the general manager of Nautilus Sports/Medical Industries, and I were in New York attending a national sporting goods show. After walking around the various displays for over an hour, we turned a corner and came face to face with Bill Kazmaier. Kazmaier is considered by many to be the world's strongest man.

For the record, Jim Flanagan stands six feet five inches, weighs 245 pounds, has shoulders that would make Arnold envious, and turns heads wherever he goes. But standing next to Bill Kazmaier, Flanagan is barely noticed. Both are nearly the same height, but Kazmaier weighs 300 pounds and looks almost twice as thick as Flanagan.

When Kazmaier met us, he was wearing a short-sleeve knit shirt. His neck looked over twenty inches and his deltoids stood out like cannonballs. But the thing that impressed me most about Bill was his massive forearms.

As I shook hands with Kazmaier, I couldn't help but remember some of the best forearms I've seen in the bodybuilding world. Mike Mentzer, Ray Mentzer, Casey Viator, Scott Wilson, and Sergio Oliva have forearms that measure from 15 to 15 9/16 inches in circumference in their best condition. And believe me, a 15-inch forearm is freakishly large, so large you'd have to see one to believe it.

"Bill," I said after we shook hands, "how big are your forearms?"

"At the World's Strongest Man Contest several years ago," he replied, "Dave Willoughby measured my right forearm at 17½ inches. I weighed 340 pounds then, so

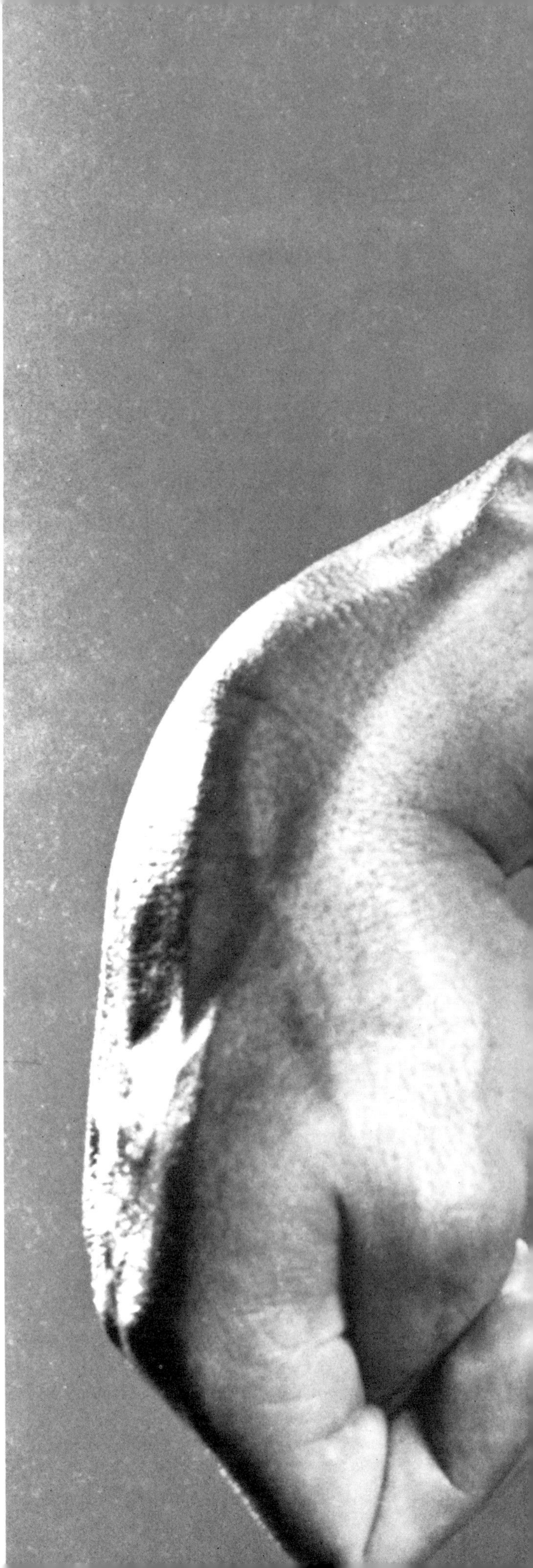

The muscular forearm of Scott Wilson.

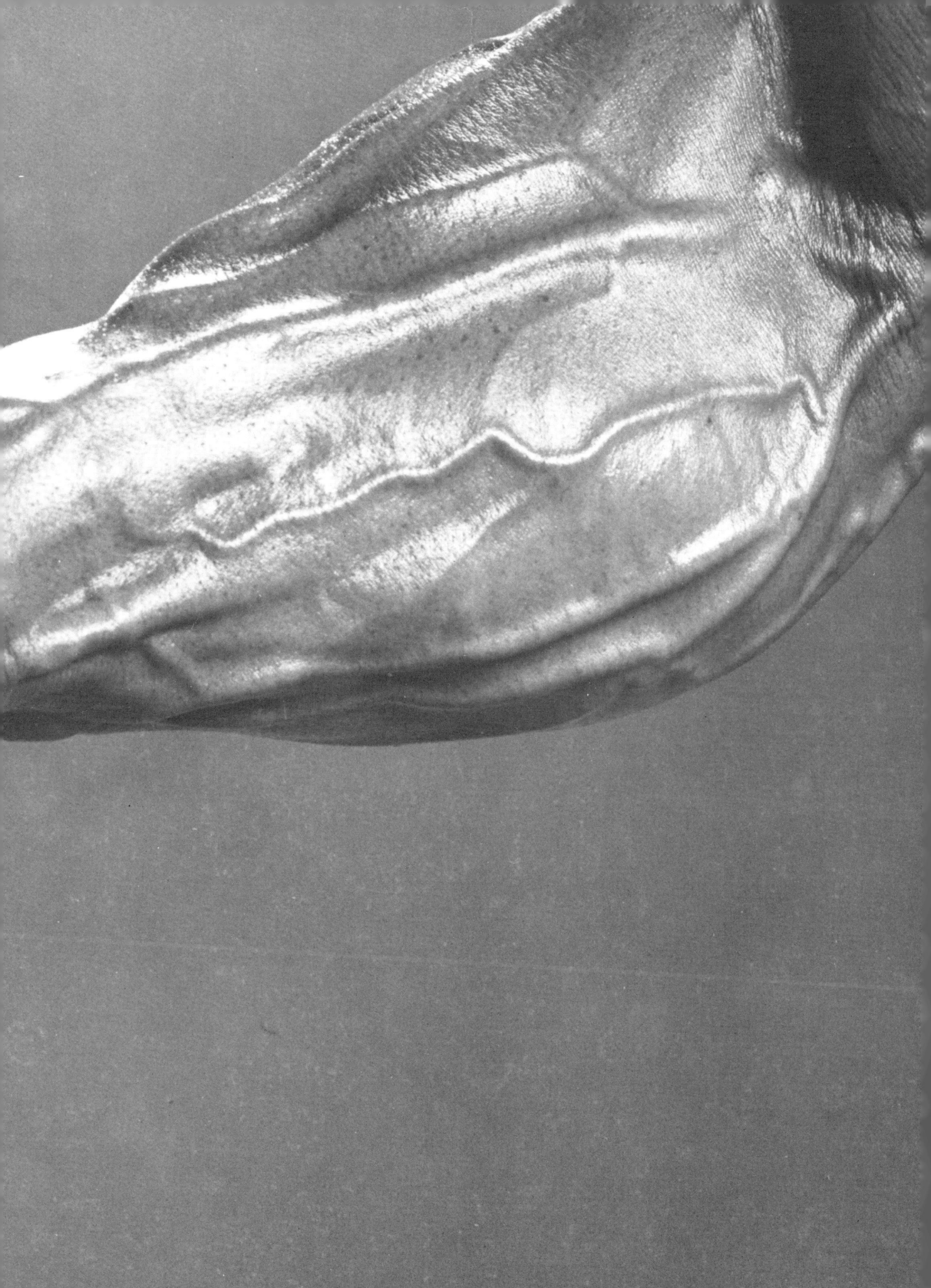

I'm sure my forearm is smaller now."

If it was smaller than 17½ inches, I couldn't tell it. Up until then, Casey Viator had the most impressive forearms I had ever seen. Not anymore. Bill Kazmaier's forearms are number one in my book and by a wide margin.

A Return to the Past

What is the secret to Bill Kazmaier's massive forearm development? Probably much of the secret goes back to the fact that Bill identifies with many of the old-time bodybuilders. He enjoys reading about the antics of the nineteenth century professional strongmen, such as Charles Vansittart, Franz "Cyclops" Bienkowski, and Louis "Apollon" Uni. These men were all noted for their exceptional hand strength. The old-timers simply were not interested in thick pectorals and sweeping lats. They were after strength, particularly of a kind easily demonstrated to their peers. Thus, grip strength and forearm size became some of the most admired traits.

While Kazmaier is well known for his world championship powerlifting abilities in the squat, bench press, and deadlift, he is also famous for his skill at lifting such things as blocks, rocks, logs, and crude, thick-handled barbells. He has competed in many strength contests in this country and abroad and is rarely defeated in any event. Much of his success is directly related to the muscular size and strength of his forearms.

Advanced Forearm Cycle

Bill Kazmaier's forearms are a result of blending the old with the new. Let's look at a forearm cycle that combines some standard exercises with some that were favored by the old-time strongmen.

1. Wrist curl with barbell, immediately followed by
2. Wrist roller, underhanded grip, immediately followed by
3. Wrist roller, overhanded grip, immediately followed by
4. Reverse curl with big-handled barbell

Wrist curl with barbell: Grasp a barbell with a palms-up grip. Rest your forearms on your thighs and the back of your hands against your knees, and be seated. Your forearms may also be placed on a declined bench for better stability. Lean forward until the angle between your upper arms and forearms is less than 90 degrees. This allows you to isolate your forearms more completely. Curl your hands smoothly and contract

---

Opposite. Tim Belknap's forearm muscles look massive from the front or the back.
Above. Tony Pearson contracts his biceps and forearms.

your forearm muscles. Pause, then lower the barbell slowly. Do not allow your forearms or torso to move. Repeat for eight to twelve repetitions. Move quickly to the wrist roller.

Wrist roller, underhanded grip: A wrist roller is a thick dowel or pipe with a cord or cable fastened through it. With barbell plates attached to the opposite end you can roll and unroll for a terrific forearm exercise.

Grasp the wrist roller with a palms-up grip. Place your wrists on a stable padded surface which is approximately four feet off the floor. With the wrist roller in your hands and in position, the barbell plates attached to the other end should barely clear the floor. Roll the cord up the handle with an alternating-hand twisting action. When the barbell plates are next to the handle, reverse the action, and lower the plates back to the floor.

If the weight is the correct amount, you won't think you'll be able to make the last foot of unrolling. Make up your mind that you can do it and you will.

Wrist roller, overhanded grip: Reduce the attached weight by 50 percent. Grasp the handles with a palms-down grip. Place your wrists back on the padded surface. Roll the cord up the handle with an alternating-hand twisting action. When at the top, lower slowly by reversing the action.

By the end of this exercise your forearms and wrists should be burning intensely. Move instantly to the reverse curl.

Reverse curl with big-handled barbell: You'll get a different feel from this exercise if you use a big-handled barbell. Your gripping muscles are much more involved. Ideally the diameter of the handle should be 2¼ inches. If a big-handled barbell is not available, try wrapping a thick towel around a standard bar.

Grasp the bar with a palms-down grip and stand erect. Stabilize your elbows against your sides and keep them there throughout the exercise. Reverse curl the barbell. Lower slowly back to the bottom. Repeat until momentary muscular failure.

Super Forearms

Your forearms should now be thoroughly pumped, pumped to a degree that you haven't experienced in the past. They will remain pumped for up to an hour. That's a definite indication that many dormant fibers were activated and fatigued.

For best results, your forearms should be worked after your upper body. Once you've completed the forearm exercise you won't be able to grip any type of barbell or dumbbell securely for at least fifteen minutes.

Give the forearm cycle a try for a month.

Gripping a normal-sized barbell handle doesn't tax your forearm muscles to the same degree as does a thick-handled barbell.

Above. Wrist curl with barbell: Flex your wrists as much as possible.
Below. Wrist roller, underhanded grip: You'll be able to use more resistance with an underhanded, rather than an overhanded, grip. If a pad is not available to support your wrists, stabilize your forearms in front of your waist.

Above. Wrist roller, overhanded grip: Make your forearm extensors beg for mercy.
Below. Reverse curl with big-handled barbell: Grasp the thick bar securely and use your biceps to force your pre-exhausted forearms to the deepest possible level of growth stimulation.

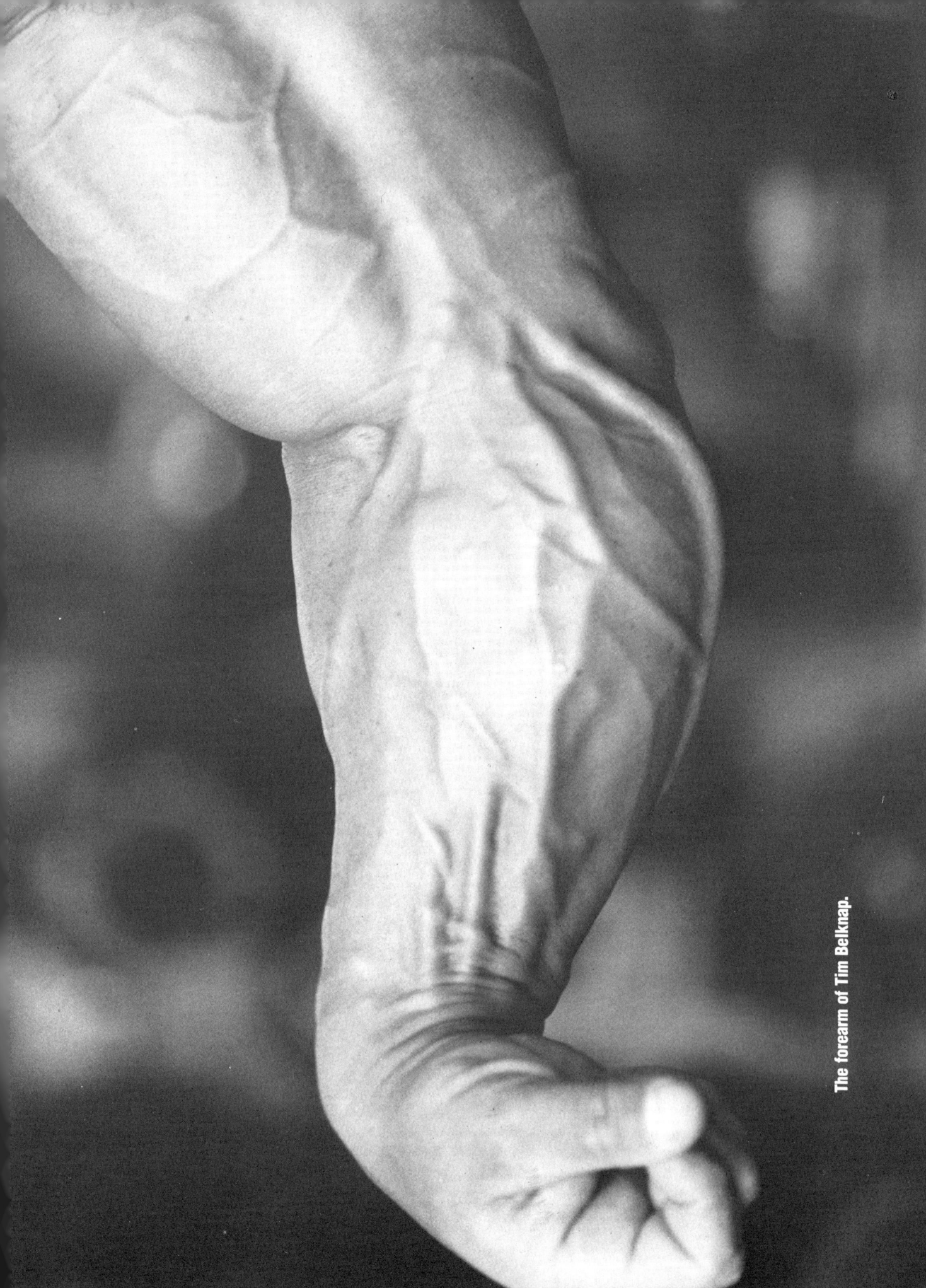

The forearm of Tim Belknap.

The top forearm measures 12 inches in circumference and bottom forearm measures 15 inches. The muscle mass of the bottom forearm, however, is over twice that of the top.

CHAPTER 11 · SUPER HIGH-INTENSITY BODYBUILDING

Stiff-legged deadlift: Stretch in the bottom position and move smoothly throughout the range of movement.

CHAPTER 11

Lower Back
Thickening Your Spinal Erectors

Chris Lund has told me repeatedly that the most complete back development—which includes upper and lower back, width and thickness, and mass and definition—belongs to the 1983 Mr. Olympia, Samir Bannout. I've never seen Bannout in person, but judging from the photographs I've seen of him, Lund's appraisal is correct. Samir's back looks superb from all angles.

If Samir has a weakness in his back—and it's really trivial to call it a weakness—it's in his lower back. His lower back could be even thicker than it is. Thicker, stronger, lower spinal erectors would improve his overall back and make the best back in the world even better.

The strongest and thickest set of lower back muscles in bodybuilding, in my opinion, belong to Casey Viator. Casey is incredibly strong on squats, leg presses, and deadlifts, and he isn't afraid to work to muscular failure on each. As a result, his lower back muscles are as thick as the barrels of two side-by-side baseball bats.

Joe Means, Most Muscular Man winner in the 1976 Mr. America contest, also has outstanding spinal erector muscles. I personally measured the depth of Joe's contracted lower back muscles at two inches. That two inches of muscle over the lower back not only looks good under the posing lights but also offers valuable strength and protection to one of the human body's most vulnerable areas.

Avoiding Sudden Movements

It is estimated that 80 percent of all bodybuilders suffer from lower back problems. Too many bodybuilders concentrate on exercises, such as bench presses, curls, and leg extensions, that do not involve the lower back. They neglect heavy exercises, such as squats, overhead presses, and deadlifts, which stress and strengthen their lower back muscles. Even the bodybuilders who do incorporate heavy squats, standing presses, and deadlifts into their routines often perform them in such a fast manner that they may actually cause back problems.

Do *not* perform any exercise—least of all exercises for your lower back—in a fast, jerky manner. Fast exercise is not only dangerous, but also unproductive.

The next time someone tells you to move quickly during exercise to produce a sudden or jerky movement against resistance just smile and walk away. The facts show that you are talking to a fool.

Sudden movements of the back are directly responsible for killing a few thousand people every year, and the backs that have been ruined by such movements number in the millions. The primary reason is whiplash!

You can get whiplash just as quickly in the lower back as you can in the neck, and the result is frequently the same. You can get a whiplash of the lower back just as easily from a power clean or a sudden deadlift as you can from a car wreck.

Controlling Force

Force is force. Your body doesn't know what the source of the force may be, and, in any case, the result is the same. Once again, the facts show that sudden movement against resistance creates an enormous level of force.

An injury is caused when a force is imposed on the body, a force that exceeds the momentary structural integrity of some part of the body. It's just that simple.

Yet, at the same time, your body requires force within reasonable levels. If the force of gravity is removed from your body for even a few days, the body reacts to this abnormal situation by starting to demineralize the bones. This reaction has created a serious problem for astronauts in the weightless environment of outer space where exercise becomes a matter of life or death.

Your muscles also require force, and they react to a lack of force by a loss of both size and strength.

So the force must be at least high enough to maintain the normal level of minerals in your bones, and it must be at least high enough to maintain the strength of your muscles. But it must not be high enough to rip your muscles out by the roots or break your bones. Sudden or jerky movements against resistance can do both.

All of these dangers can be avoided by the use of common sense, which often seems to be in short supply in some circles in the field of exercise.

High levels of force caused by a sudden movement are probably responsible for almost 100 percent of the injuries produced by exercise. Properly performed exercise can and will go a long way in the direction of preventing injuries. Improperly performed exercise, which usually means sudden movement against resis-

Notice the thickness of Mark Marshall's lower back muscles.

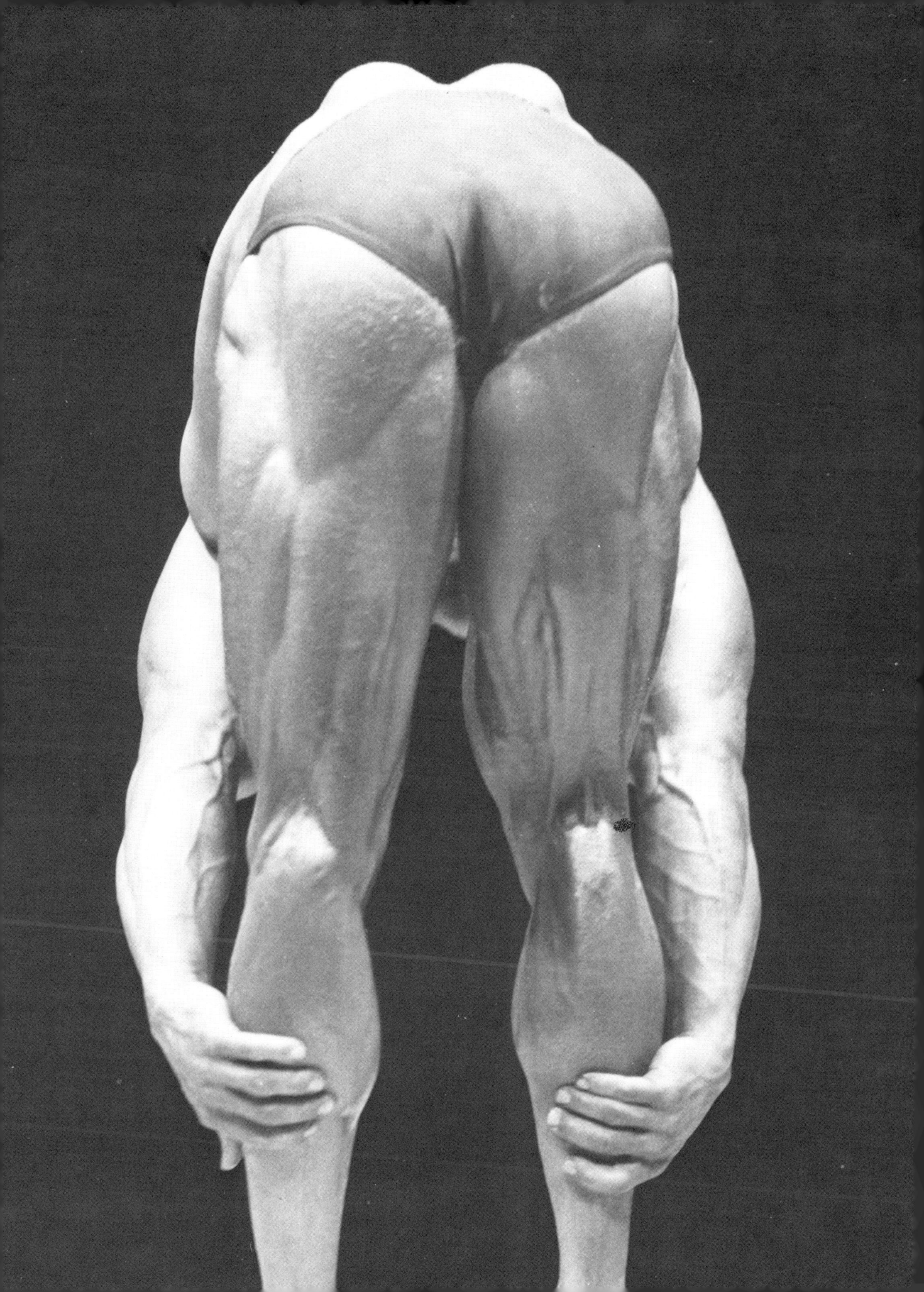

Shown is a four-phase sequence of Tom Platz performing deadlifts.

tance, will eventually hurt you.

These facts apply to every muscle producing movement in your body, and they are particularly important in regard to the muscles of your lower back.

Lower Back Cycle

The specialized, lower-back cycle, when properly performed, is both safe and productive. It involves only two exercises, one with a machine and the other with a barbell.

1. Nautilus lower back machine, breakdowns, immediately followed by
2. Stiff-legged deadlift with barbell

Nautilus lower back machine: This machine, according to Arthur Jones, is the most important machine he has ever produced because it provides direct, rotary resistance to the lower back muscles without compression force being applied to the spinal column. In other words, the effective force is always 180 degrees opposite the direction of movement of your torso. This is not possible with a barbell exercise.

Enter the machine from the side by straddling the seat. Make sure you are seated on the seat bottom, not the angle between the seat bottom and the seat back. Your back should be underneath the highest roller pad. Stabilize your lower body by moving your thighs under the bottom roller pads. Place your feet firmly on the platform. Fasten the seat belt around your hips and interlace your fingers across your waist. Move your torso backward smoothly until it is in line with your thighs. Pause in the contracted position. Return slowly to the starting position and repeat for eight to twelve repetitions.

Have your training partner immediately reduce the resistance by 10 percent. This should permit you to perform another three repetitions. After the three repetitions, again have your partner remove approximately 10 percent from the weight stack. Continue doing smooth repetitions until muscular failure. Do not jerk the movement arm. Keep the movements slow and controlled. Your lower back should be burning as you move to the stiff-legged deadlift.

Stiff-legged deadlift: The deadlift will bring into action your lats and hamstrings to force your lower back to a deeper level of growth stimulation. A small platform should be used to increase the range of movement.

Stand on the platform and grasp the barbell with an under-and-over grip. Your feet should be under the bar. Lift the barbell to the standing position. Keeping your knees locked, the barbell should be lowered to the stretched position and smoothly lifted back to the top. Repeat for twelve to fifteen repetitions.

Good Advice

Specialize on your lower back and make it one of your best body parts. Perform all your repetitions smoothly and slowly. Avoid fast movements. Train harder and briefer. Treat your lower back with care and respect, and it will reward you with vitality and strength.

Nautilus lower back machine: Move under control and pause in the contracted position.
Opposite. **The superb back of Mike Christian.**

CHAPTER 12
SUPER HIGH-INTENSITY BODYBUILDING

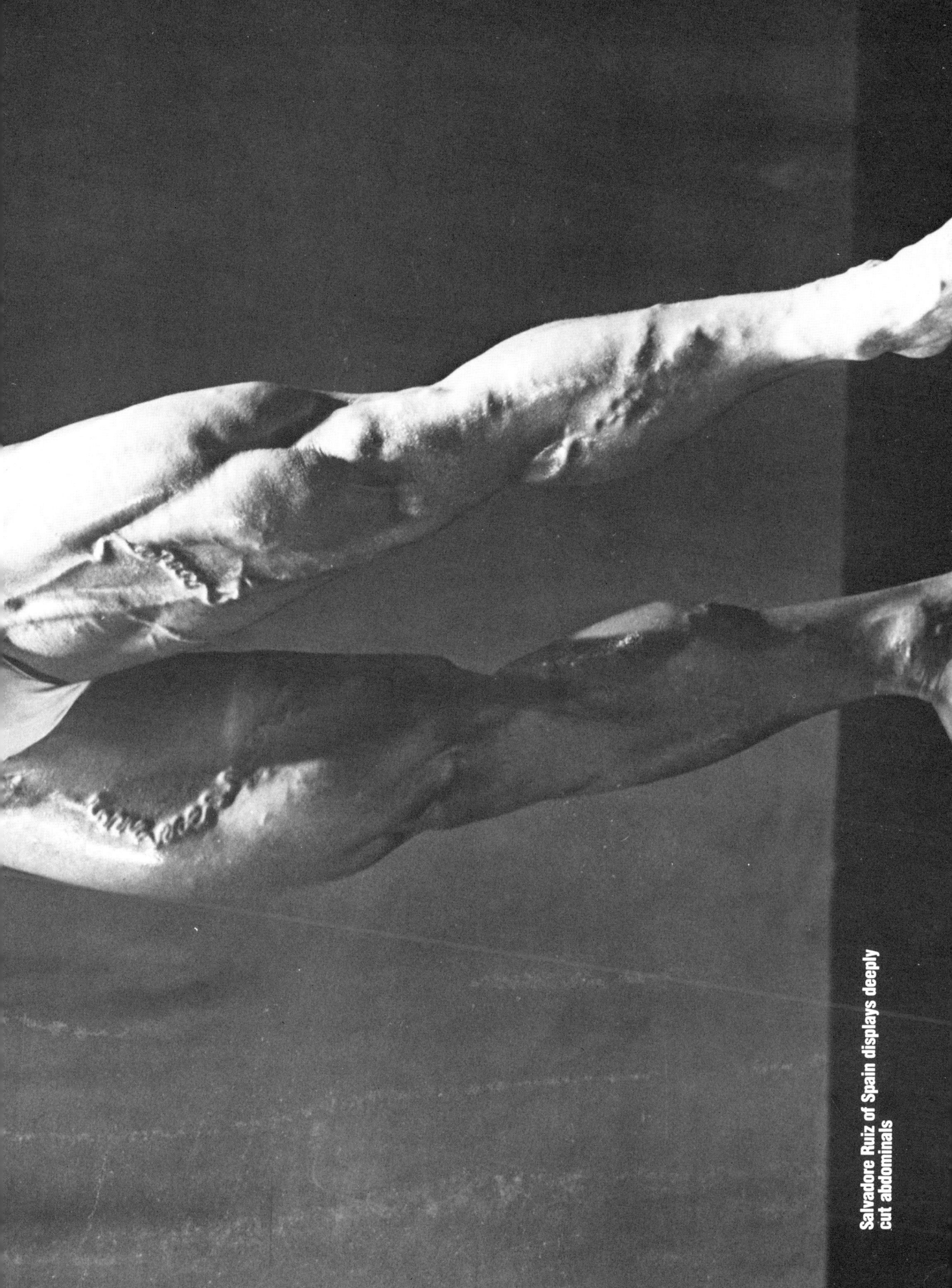

Salvadore Ruiz of Spain displays deeply cut abdominals

CHAPTER 12

Waist: Ripping Your Abdominals

A successful bodybuilder must have a low level of fat between his or her skin and muscles. When a bodybuilder with a low level of fat contracts muscles, the muscular development is easy to see and the surface veins become larger and more prominent. Thus, the combination of a low level of fat, outstanding muscular development, and prominent surface veins has become known as "ripped."

Clarence Bass, Most Muscular winner in the Mr. America Past 40 contest, is well known for his ripped physique. In fact, he's written two successful books, *Ripped* and *Ripped 2*, on the subject of getting lean and staying lean.

Over twenty-nine months, Clarence had his percentage of body fat measured twenty-one times by scientists at the Lovelace Medical Center in Albuquerque, New Mexico. The scientists in New Mexico measured his body fat by weighing him both in air and in water. Since the specific gravity of muscle and fat are different (muscle is denser than fat), the difference between the air and water bodyweight weighings can be used to calculate the percentage of body fat.

Underwater weighings are considered to be the most accurate and reliable method of calculating body fat. Thousands of athletes and nonathletes have been measured using this technique in research laboratories throughout the United States, and standards have been established.

For example, the average American woman's body fat level is 27 percent. The average man's is 15 percent. Most male college athletes, depending on the sport, measure from 8 to 14 percent. Marathon runners rate 6 percent.

Clarence Bass's body fat over twenty-nine months averaged 3.7 percent. His lowest level was 2.4 percent on two separate occasions.

You'd think that 2.4 percent is about as low as you can go and still remain healthy, since you do need a small amount of body fat to function properly. But in February, 1985, I saw some pictures of a Canadian bodybuilder who defies belief. If Clarence Bass is ripped, then this guy is super ripped. His body fat must be in the neighborhood of 0.4 percent, and he appears to be in excellent health.

The Canadian's name is Mike Watson. He is five feet seven inches tall and weighs 180 pounds in his leanest condition. Watson placed second in his weight class at the 1984 Mr. Canada contest, but according to Chris Lund, he should have won. The photos of Mike in this chapter were taken in 1985, and they prove him to be the most ripped bodybuilder that I've ever seen.

Few bodybuilders have the potential to be ripped like Mike Watson. To learn why requires an understanding of three factors: (1) genetics, (2) reduced-calorie dieting, and (3) proper exercise.

Genetics

Where you store fat and to what degree are mostly genetic, in that they are inherited from your ancestors. Just as different families and different races have characteristic heights, coloring, and nose shapes, they may also have characteristic patterns of fat distribution.

Men, for example, tend to deposit their fat more frontally than do women. Women tend to deposit their fat more on the back of the body.

People with dark eyes, dark hair, and dark skin usually have fewer fat cells than those who have blue eyes, blond hair, and pale skin. Fewer fat cells means a greater potential for leanness. Ninety percent of the most muscular and ripped bodybuilding champions today are dark-eyed and dark-skinned.

Furthermore, most champion bodybuilders do *not* store fat in disproportionally large amounts around their waists. They tend to store it more evenly throughout their bodies. So when they lose fat they tend to lose it in a proportionate manner.

Most people are just the opposite. They have certain spots, especially around the midsection, that seem to attract fat. They can shrink this fat, but it's usually the last to go—and it goes with great difficulty.

Certain people also have different ordering of favorite fat-storage spots. But there is most definitely an ordering, and that ordering is genetically determined and not subject to alteration.

Genetic qualities are limiting factors, but this is not to say that you cannot improve your existing appearance. With strict attention paid to your diet and exercise you can reach the upper limits of your genetic potential.

Some of the best abdominals in the business: (*Opposite*) Tony Pearson, (*Overleaf*) Lee Haney, Berry DeMey, Bill Grant, Robby Robinson, Chuck Williams, and Jesup Wilkcoz.

Lee Haney

Berry DeMey

Bill Grant

Robby Robinson

Chuck Williams

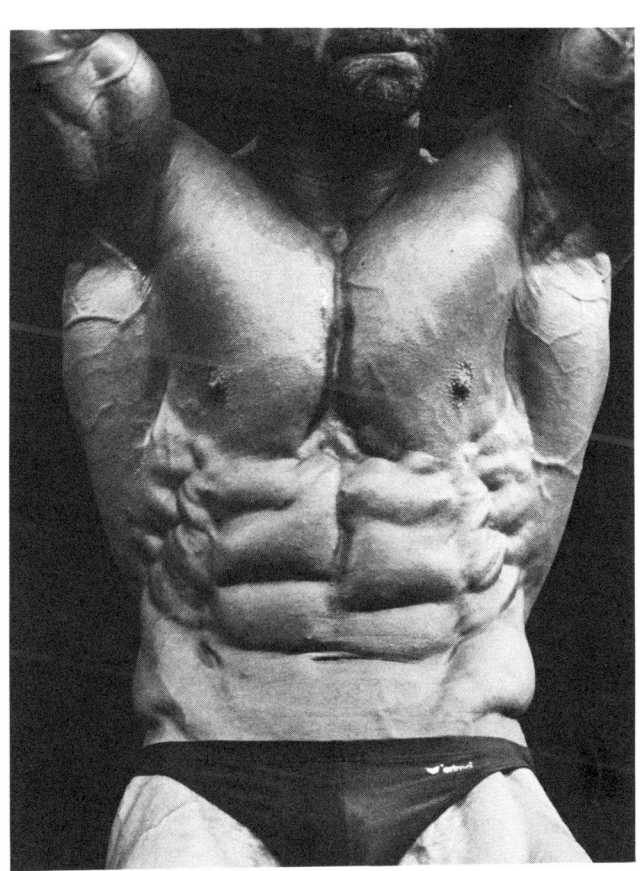
Jesup Wilkcoz

Reduced-Calorie Dieting

Losing fat is a result of your calorie intake and calorie output. Generally, your calorie intake must be less than your calorie output. You must eat fewer calories than you expend on a daily basis.

The key to losing fat—and making sure that what you lose is fat, not muscle—is to reduce your calories gradually. To estimate the number of calories that you need per day to lose fat gradually, follow the guidelines given below. (Note that these guidelines apply best to young men between the ages of 20 to 40 who are no more than fifteen pounds overfat.)

1. Multiply your bodyweight in pounds by ten. This will provide you with an estimate of the number of calories you need to consume each day to lose fat effectively. There are 3,500 calories in one pound of body fat. Thus, a reduction of 1,000 dietary calories a day below your regular calorie consumption will result in a minus 7,000 calories (1,000 × 7) per week, or a loss of two pounds.
2. Select a calorie listing from the chart that is nearest to that number. (See page 156.)
3. Apply the appropriate listings to your daily meal planning.
4. Adhere to the meal planning for one week and record your weight loss. Ideally, the loss should be two pounds. If your weight loss exceeds two pounds the first week, then raise your daily calories. If your weight loss is less than two pounds, reduce your calories to the next-lowest level.

Proper Exercise

Intense exercise for your midsection will stimulate the involved muscles to grow larger and stronger. But such exercise will not burn the fat cells that overlie the exercised muscles.

The fat that is stored around your waist is in a form called lipids. To be used as energy, the lipids must be converted to fatty acids. This is a very complex chemical procedure. To be used as fuel, the lipids must travel through the bloodstream to the liver. In the liver they must be converted to fatty acids, which are then transported to the working muscles.

This is well and good. But a problem arises because there are no direct pathways from the fat cells to the muscle cells. When fat is used for energy, it is mobilized primarily through the liver out of the multiple fat cells all over the body. And that selection process that your body uses for mobilizing its fat stores is programmed by your genes.

Thus, spot reducing of fatty deposits around your waistline is not possible. The fat comes off gradually from throughout your body, not just a few spots. But spot producing of muscle mass is possible. And developing your abdominal, oblique, and surrounding muscles will certainly help you attain that ripped look once you've significantly reduced your percentage of body fat.

The ripped-to-the-bone physique of Mike Watson.

Advanced Midsection Cycle

The following three exercises should be performed as described:

1. Trunk curl on floor, immediately followed by
2. Hanging leg raise, immediately followed by
3. Side bend with dumbbell

Trunk curl on floor: This exercise activates your rectus abdominis by relaxing your iliopsoas muscles. Lie face up on the floor with your hands behind your head. Keep your chin on your chest. Bring your heels up close to your buttocks and spread your knees. Do not anchor your feet under anything, and don't have a partner hold your knees down. Anchoring the feet brings into action other muscles.

Try to curl your trunk smoothly to a sitting position. Only one third of a standard sit-up can be done in this fashion. Pause in the contracted position and lower your trunk slowly to the floor. Repeat until positive muscular failure. When twelve or more repetitions can be accomplished, add a barbell plate behind your head. Move immediately to the hanging leg raise.

Hanging leg raise: The trunk curl effectively isolates your rectus abdominis muscles. The leg raise involves your iliopsoas or hip flexors, as well as your lats, to force your pre-exhausted abdominals to deeper levels of fatigue.

Hang on to an overhead bar. Your hands should be shoulder-width apart. Raise your legs smoothly and touch your toes to the bar. Lower your legs slowly to the bottom position. Do not bend your arms during the raising or lowering. Keep them straight throughout the movement. Repeat for eight to twelve repetitions. Move without resting to the side bend.

Side bend: Grasp a heavy dumbbell in your right hand. Stand erect and place your left hand on top of your head. Bend laterally to your right. This bending works your left oblique muscles. Return smoothly to the erect position. Repeat the bending to your right for twelve repetitions. Switch the dumbbell to your left hand and perform twelve lateral bends to your left side.

Mike Watson does concentration curls in Champion's Gym in Hamilton, Ontario.

Opposite. The leanness and vascularity of Watson's legs lead me to believe that his body fat percentage is as close to zero as it is possible to get and still be healthy.

Important Advice

Contrary to popular belief, the muscles of your midsection should be trained in exactly the same manner as your other muscles: one set of several exercises performed slowly and smoothly for eight to twelve repetitions, repeated no more than three times weekly. This is the most efficient way to larger, stronger muscles—and larger, stronger midsection muscles are one requirement for that ripped look. The other requirement involves reducing your percentage of body fat through a gradual reduction of dietary calories.

Give both the recommended diet and exercise program your best shot, and in less than a month, you should see and feel the difference. Get started today!

Daily Guidelines for Losing Fat Using the Four Food Groups

FOOD	For 1,400 Calories	For 1,500 Calories	For 1,600 Calories	For 1,700 Calories	For 1,800 Calories	For 1,900 Calories	For 2,000 Calories	For 2,100 Calories	For 2,200 Calories	NOTES
Meat Group	3 Servings (or a total of 7 ounces cooked wt.)	3 Servings (or a total of 7 ounces cooked wt.)	3 Servings (or a total of 7 ounces cooked wt.)	3 Servings (or a total of 7 ounces cooked wt.)	3+ Servings (or a total of 9 ounces cooked wt.)	4 Servings (or a total of 10 ounces cooked wt.)	4 Servings (or a total of 10 ounces cooked wt.)	4 Servings (or a total of 10 ounces cooked wt.)	4+ Servings (or a total of 12 ounces cooked wt.)	Choose lean, well-trimmed meats: beef, veal, lamb, pork. Poultry and fish should have skin removed. One egg can be substituted for 1 serving of meat. One ounce lean meat = 60 calories.
Milk Group	1 cup of skim milk, 1 cup of whole milk	2 cups of whole milk	2 cups of whole milk	2 cups of whole milk, 1 cup of skim milk	2 cups of whole milk, 1 cup of skim milk	2 cups of whole milk, 1 cup of skim milk	2 cups of whole milk, 2 cups of skim milk	2 cups of whole milk, 2 cups of skim milk	2 cups of whole milk, 2 cups of skim milk	Two cups milk means two 8-ounce measuring cups. One cup skim milk = 100 calories. One cup whole milk = 150 calories.
Fruits and Vegetables Group	4 Servings	4 Servings	5 Servings	5 Servings	6 Servings	6 Servings	6 Servings	6 Servings	6 Servings	One fruit serving = 1 medium fruit, 2 small fruits, ½ banana, ¼ cantaloupe, 10–12 grapes or cherries, 1 cup fresh berries or ½ cup fresh, canned or frozen unsweetened fruit or fruit juice. Include one citrus fruit or other good source of vitamin C daily. One fruit or vegetable serving = 50–75 calories. 1 vegetable serving = ½ cup cooked or 1 cup raw leafy vegetable. Include one dark green or deep yellow vegetable or other good source of vitamin A at least every other day.
Bread and Cereal Group	4½ Servings	5 Servings	6 Servings	6 Servings	6 Servings	6 Servings	6 Servings	7 Servings	7 Servings	One serving = 1 slice bread; 1 small dinner roll; ½ cup cooked cereal, noodles, macaroni, spaghetti, rice, cornmeal; 1 ounce (about 1 cup) ready-to-eat unsweetened iron-fortified cereal. One bread/cereal serving = 75 calories.
Other Foods	2½ Servings	3 Servings	3 Servings	3 Servings	3 Servings	3 Servings	3 Servings	4 Servings	4 Servings	1 serving = 1 teaspoon butter, margarine, or oil; 6 nuts; 2 teaspoons salad dressing or 35 calories or less of another food.

Above, left. Cory Everson has not neglected her waistline. *Above, right.* Mr. Olympia Frank Zane displays his championship abdominals. *Below.* Since spot reducing of fat is impossible, any exercise for your upper or lower body will contribute to the loss of fat around your waist. *Overleaf.* Canadian bodybuilders Mark Bolduc and Serge Morreux pose their rock-hard abdominals.

CHAPTER 13
SUPER HIGH-INTENSITY BODYBUILDING

According to Chris Lund, David and Peter Paul are some of the very few bodybuilders at Gold's Gym in Venice, California, who do heavy neck work.

CHAPTER 13

Neck: Expanding Your Collar

"Mickey has the biggest neck I've ever seen," I said to Terry Todd, an old friend from Texas and former super heavyweight powerlifting champion. Terry, who is an authority on strength history, was visiting Florida and we were driving from Lake Helen to Ocala to meet with Arthur Jones. As we approached Jones's ranch in Ocala, Terry kept asking questions about Mickey.

"Exactly how big is his neck?"

"Jones measured it last summer at thirty-three inches," I replied.

"Thirty-three inches," Terry mumbled, shaking his head.

"It's probably bigger now. He's added at least twenty pounds since then," I commented.

"What does he weigh?" Todd asked.

"About 380 pounds," I answered, "but Arthur says he has the genetic potential to weigh even more, perhaps a hundred pounds more, without getting overfat."

"Damn," said Terry as he kept shaking his head in amazement. "How strong is he?"

"That's hard to say," I replied; "Jones has never really tested him in an all-out effort. But I can tell you this: Three Tampa Buccaneer football players, each weighing over 250 pounds, were watching him train several months ago. All of a sudden, Mickey turned around and threw a series of forearm shivers against a concrete wall with such force that the whole wall shook. Everybody in the room jumped back, headed for the door, and ran to the nearest rest room to empty their pants. There's no doubt in my mind that Mickey could have taken on all three of those offensive linemen from the Tampa Bay football team and come out on top."

"Mickey! I can't wait to see him," Terry said, smiling, as we pulled into Jones's JumboLair Ranch.

JumboLair is located on seven hundred acres of land in the heart of central Florida. Other ranches in the area raise cattle and horses, but Jones's ranch specializes in exotic animals: crocodiles, alligators, poisonous snakes, giant tortoises, rhinos, elephants, and a gorilla—a gorilla named Mickey! Mickey is eighteen years old. He was raised by Barnum and Bailey Circus until Jones purchased him in 1984, and he does indeed weigh 380 pounds and have a neck that measures 33 inches. Some of his other measurements include a 54-inch chest, 17-inch forearms, and 13-inch wrists.

Mickey's neck, however, in my opinion, is his outstanding body part.

"Wow," said Terry Todd as we caught sight of Mickey in his cage. "He's gargantuan."

From the front, Mickey's neck size is less evident. Only from the side can you appreciate the foot-thick trapezius muscles that seem to start in the middle of his back and run to the top of his head.

"Before I saw Mickey," I said to Terry, "I would have never believed that a gorilla's neck would grow that large. But after seeing him in the flesh, I believe it

---

Mr. Olympia Lee Haney has not ignored his neck.

because it actually looks larger than thirty-three inches."

"You're right," noted Todd. "I wonder which lifter, wrestler, or football player has come the closest to building such a colossal neck?"

"The closest I've seen to Mickey's neck in a human belonged to a football player I knew at Baylor University in 1962 and '63," I ventured. "His name was Bobby Crenshaw. Crenshaw stood about six feet three inches, weighed about 240, and wore a burr haircut. Sitting behind him in several classes, you couldn't help but notice the rippling muscle on the back of his neck. Crenshaw had a similar development to Mickey, one that seemed to start halfway down his back and stretch to above his ears."

"How big was Crenshaw's neck?" Terry asked.

"I'd say it was every bit of twenty-one inches. But it wasn't the sheer size of Crenshaw's neck that was so impressive. It was the muscular formation and thickness that he had on the back of his head and neck. And it's the same with Mickey . . . you know what I mean?"

"Yes, I do," Terry answered, nodding his head. "Judging from pictures I've seen, some of the old-time strongmen and wrestlers had that same type of neck thickness. Men such as George Hackenschmidt, Stanislaus Z, Karl Swoboda, and Gama. Not only were they adept at lifting heavy weights of various types, but they were champion wrestlers."

"Milo Steinborn was in that category, too," I noted. "And Milo, judging from some of the old pictures I've seen of him, certainly knew how to pose his neck to make it appear even bigger than it was.

"Speaking of posing," I continued, "of the present-day bodybuilders, my pick for the best neck goes to Bill Richardson, a Mr. Universe winner from England. Richardson is one of the few champion bodybuilders who emphasizes his neck. Most of his contemporaries ignore their necks altogether."

"It's a shame too," commented Terry, "because a thick, fully developed neck sets a man apart from his peers. A large neck has always been a symbol of strength and virility. In a way, it establishes a person's physical superiority almost immediately."

"Sorta the opposite of the way Mickey makes us feel, wouldn't you say?" I responded.

Terry again nodded and we both smiled. We'd been observing Mickey for at least thirty minutes, and it was time to move on and see some of the other animals on Jones's ranch. Mickey appeared to appreciate our admiration. He seemed to bid us goodbye as we walked away.

Perhaps he understood. Perhaps he knew that both Terry Todd and I, at that moment, wished we could have that mound of muscle surrounding our necks,

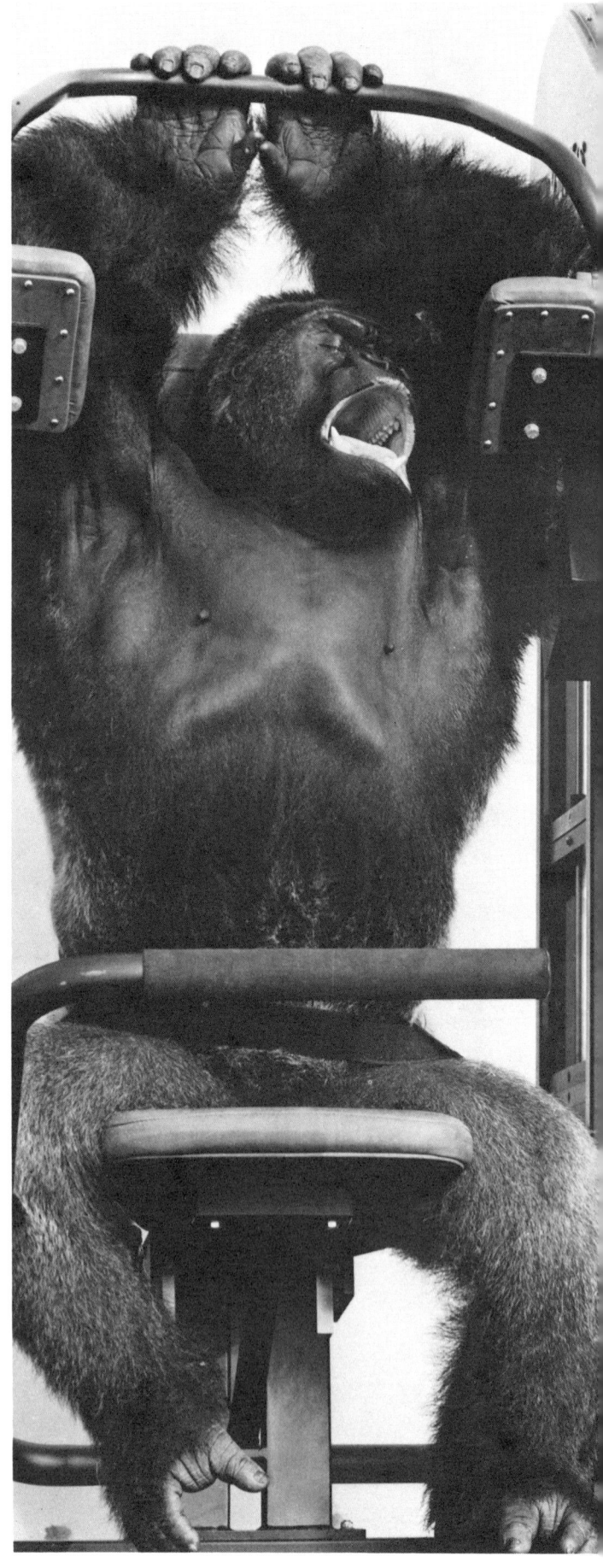

Mickey, Arthur Jones's 380-pound gorilla, is shown in the stretched position of the Nautilus pullover machine.
Opposite. Only from the side can the mass of Mickey's neck be seen.

even if for only a day.

Although I can't speak for Terry, I know that since that day at the JumboLair Ranch, I've worked my neck a little harder than I had in the past. Thanks, Mickey!

Advanced Neck Cycle

Football players and wrestlers frequently use the neck bridge as the primary exercise for working their necks. While the neck bridge does indeed work the neck, it does so by providing potentially dangerous compression forces on the cervical spine. And the neck bridge does not work as adequately the front and sides of the neck as it does the back. A far more efficient and effective exercise for the neck is performed on the Nautilus 4-way neck machine. The other important neck exercise is the shoulder shrug. The neck cycle, therefore, involves only two exercises:

1. Nautilus 4-way neck machine, negative forced, immediately followed by
2. Shoulder shrug with barbell, breakdowns

Nautilus 4-way neck machine, negative forced: This machine provides comfortable, safe, direct exercise for the important neck muscles in four different directions: back, front, left side, and right side.

Back extension: Sit in the machine with the back of your head next to the movement arm. Adjust your seat height until the back of your head is squarely in the middle of the pads when you are seated erectly. Extend your head as far back as possible. Pause. Return slowly to the stretched position. Repeat for eight to twelve repetitions. Do several negative-forced repetitions by using your arm to assist you in the positive movement. From the seated position, place one hand on the top of the head pads and push backward. Remove your hand and stabilize yourself in the extended position. Perform a slow negative repetition. Repeat the negative-forced movement three times.

Front flexion: Turn and face the machine. Your nose should now be in the center of the pads. Stabilize your torso by lightly grasping the handles. Move your head smoothly toward your chest. Pause. Return slowly to stretched position. Repeat for eight to twelve repetitions. Do three negative-forced repetitions by using one arm to assist you in doing the positive work.

Lateral contraction: Turn your body in the machine until your left ear is in the center of the pads. Stabilize

Above. Don Ross gives us his famous most muscular pose. Don is a big believer in neck training.
Below. Nautilus 4-way neck machine, back extension: Lower the movement arm under control to the stretched position.
Opposite. Bill Richardson's neck is the most perfectly developed of present-day bodybuilders.
Overleaf, left. Lee Haney performs a combination upright row and shoulder shrug from a behind-the-back position.
Overleaf, right. Shoulder shrug with barbell: Raise the barbell smoothly, pause, and lower it slowly.

your torso by lightly grasping the handles. Move your head toward your left shoulder. Pause. Keep your shoulders square. Return slowly to the stretched position. Repeat for eight to twelve repetitions. Do three negative-forced repetitions by using your left arm to pull the movement arm into the contracted position. Reverse the procedure for lateral contraction to the right side.

Shoulder shrug with barbell, breakdowns: Grasp a heavy barbell with an under-and-over grip. Wrist straps may also be employed for a more secure hold. The barbell should be loaded so assistants can reduce the weight by 20 percent twice.

Stand with the barbell hanging at arms' length. Shrug your shoulders smoothly and try to touch them to your ears. Pause. Lower slowly to the bottom. Repeat for eight to twelve repetitions. Without putting the barbell down, have your assistants at either end of the barbell strip 20 percent off. Perform a few more smooth, slow repetitions. When you are unable to shrug to the top position, have them remove another 20 percent. Continue doing repetitions with this weight until failure.

Keeping Inspired

Proper use of the 4-way neck machine and the shoulder shrug will thoroughly congest your neck musculature. In fact, your neck circumference should be pumped by at least one inch.

For your benefit, however, work into the neck cycle gradually. Going into it full blast will leave you with a very sore neck for a week.

Train your neck at the end of your workout twice a week for the next month. Your neck will quickly respond by growing larger and stronger, and all your shirt collars will fit tighter—or won't fit at all!

When you feel like you've reached a plateau in training your neck, or if you've simply become a little complacent in working your neck, why not plan a brief vacation to central Florida? With a little luck, you just might get to visit my friend Mickey. After visiting Mickey, I'll guarantee that you'll be inspired to work your neck a lot harder.

T-bar rows work your trapezius as well as your biceps and lats.

CHAPTER 14 · SUPER HIGH-INTENSITY BODYBUILDING

Barbarian style bench pressing with 495 pounds. Note the reverse grip.

Chapter 14

Problems: Answering Your Questions

Stage Repetitions

Q. *I'm fascinated with stage repetitions. What makes them so result-producing?*

A. Stage repetitions are result-producing because they tend to improve most bodybuilders' strength curves. Most trainees who have lifted barbells for a number of years have very peaked strength curves in all their major muscle groups.

In the barbell curl, for example, they are strong in the middle and weak at the beginning and at the end. Their strength curve during a curl resembles a peaked mountain.

Stage repetitions, by isolating three different sections of the curl, tend to flatten out the peaked curve. By flattening out your strength curve, you are working more of the involved muscle fibers at the start and at the end of an exercise. And more muscle fiber involvement means greater growth stimulation.

Substituting Full Squats

Q. *Can I substitute the full squat for the sissy squat in Chapter 4?*

A. Yes, you may make this substitution. But in doing so, I'd also change the order of the exercises to the following:

1. Leg curl, 1¼ system, immediately followed by
2. Leg extension, 1¼ system, immediately followed by
3. Full squat with barbell

Doing the leg extension immediately before the full squat will make the squat harder and thus more productive.

Calf Raises

Q. *What about varying the feet position (toes in and toes out) on the calf raise? Is this advantageous?*

A. Yes, there is some benefit to changing your feet position. Generally, most people can contract their gastrocnemius muscles best in a standing position by turning their toes out and their heels in. On the other hand, they can stretch these muscles best by turning their toes in and their heels out. Keeping your feet straight ahead and parallel to each other seems to involve the best of both extremes.

The most important rules in working your calves are not related to the positioning of your feet; rather, they are concerned with proper form:

1. Make sure you keep your knees locked throughout the entire movement. Unlocking your knees even slightly removes some of the resistance from your calves and makes the exercise easier.
2. Concentrate on performing the range of movement smoothly and slowly with a pause at both ends.

Q. *Should calf raises be done barefoot or with shoes on?*

A. It is more comfortable on your feet to do calf raises while wearing some type of flexible athletic shoes. I see no advantage in doing the exercise barefoot.

Nautilus Pullover Machine

Q. *Occasionally I read in muscle magazines that the Nautilus pullover machine does not build bulk. Is that correct?*

A. The idea that the Nautilus pullover machine does not build bulk is ridiculous. If bulk is defined as increased muscular size and strength, then any exercise, or exercise machine, that can be performed in a progressive manner will contribute to the building of bulk. For a number of reasons, the Nautilus pullover machine is a superior form of progressive exercise. It provides:

1. Direct resistance for your latissimus dorsi muscles rather than filtering it through your weaker arm muscles.
2. Rotary movement, which allows you to stretch the lats in the extended position and contract them fully in the flexed position.
3. Balanced, variable resistance, which contributes to full-range muscle fiber involvement.

According to Arthur Jones, this photo that he took of Sergio Oliva in 1971 is the only picture he has ever seen where the width of a man's flexed upper arms exceeds the height of his head. In other words, Sergio's right or left arm is actually wider than his head is high. Jones says that such an arm-to-head ratio has never been duplicated by any other bodybuilder.

Wide-Grip Bench Presses

Q. *Is it okay to use a wide-grip bench press in the chest cycle instead of a medium-grip bench press?*

A. No! Taking a wide grip on the bench press shortens your range of movement around your shoulders and makes the exercise easier. If in doubt about your hand spacing, always choose the hand spacing that allows for the greatest range of movement. A shoulder-width hand spacing on the bench press adds 20 percent or more to the range of movement that you would get using a wide, collar-to-collar grip. Always look for ways to make your exercises harder, not easier, and your results will be much more productive.

Slow Versus Fast Chin-Ups

Q. *Are slow chin-ups better than fast chin-ups?*

A. Absolutely! Chin-ups done slowly isolate the involved muscles more thoroughly and more intensely than do fast chin-ups. You can prove this to yourself by performing only one repetition in the chin-up. The catch, however, is to do the positive and the negative phases as slowly as possible. Try to take 30 to 40 seconds to pull up, and another 30 to 40 seconds to lower yourself. It won't take you very long to realize the muscle-building effect of slow movements.

Building the Wrists

Q. *Will the recommended exercises for the forearms also build my wrists?*

A. Exercise for your forearms will build your wrists, but not to the same degree as your forearms. The reason is that there are no muscles in your wrists. The changeable components of your wrists are tendons and bones, and tendons and bones do not have the same potential for growth as do your muscles. For example, specializing on your forearms for a month might add a half-inch of muscle mass on the circumference of each of your contracted forearms. If such is the case, you might also add one-sixteenth of an inch to the circumference of each wrist.

High-Repetition Sit-Ups

Q. *I like to do several hundred sit-ups a day for my waist. Will this interfere with my high-intensity training?*

A. If you've developed a certain tolerance for doing several hundred sit-ups a day, then it may not interfere with your training. But it certainly will do nothing to facilitate building the muscles of your midsection. Developing the muscles of your midsection, or any muscle of your body, requires that the exercise be high in intensity. High in intensity is best defined as working to momentary muscular failure, *which failure should oc-*

Bertil Fox.

Opposite, above. Tom Platz is an advocate of full squats.
Opposite, below. Mike Christian does leg presses.
Overleaf. Slow repetitions are always more productive from a muscle-building standpoint than fast repetitions.

cur between eight and twelve repetitions. Performing several hundred sit-ups is an indication that the exercise is low in intensity. Low-intensity exercise is of little value in bodybuilding.

Heavy Side Bends

Q. *I've always heard that side bends with a heavy weight would broaden the waist. What about it?*

A. It is true that exercise will broaden a muscle. But in my twenty-five years of bodybuilding, I've never seen a single bodybuilder who had waist muscles that were too wide. I've seen many that had waists that were too broad, but they were to broad from fat, not muscle.

Do not be afraid of working your oblique and abdominal muscles with heavy weights. If you ever got these muscles too broad, which is very unlikely, all you'd have to do is simply stop working them for several weeks and you'd get an automatic reduction in their size. Atrophy is all too easy to achieve.

Gaining Weight

Q. *What do you recommend for gaining bodyweight?*

A. Assuming that you want the additional bodyweight to be muscle, and not fat, then I recommend the following:

1. High-intensity exercise as described in this book.
2. Adequate rest for your specific needs, which usually includes six to nine hours of sleep a night.
3. Well-balanced nutrition composed of daily servings of the four basic food groups: meat, dairy products, fruits and vegetables, and breads and cereals.

The first two factors are far more important in building muscle mass than the third factor. But for over thirty years bodybuilders have been brainwashed to believe that building muscle is at least 80 percent diet and nutrition. Upon hearing this time and time again, Arthur Jones frequently says, "Instead of being 80 percent, bodybuilding is 100 percent nutrition—but only if you don't eat. Just try going without food for a week and see what happens to your body!"

Protein Requirement

Q. *How much protein do I need a day to build muscle mass?*

A. Probably not nearly as much as you have been led to believe. To understand why, you need to know that more than 70 percent of muscle is water. Only 22 percent of muscle is protein.

And I know that you frequently read that over 90 percent of muscle is protein. But where do you read this information? In muscle magazines, which muscle magazines happen also to sell protein supplements.

Multiple research studies have proved that American

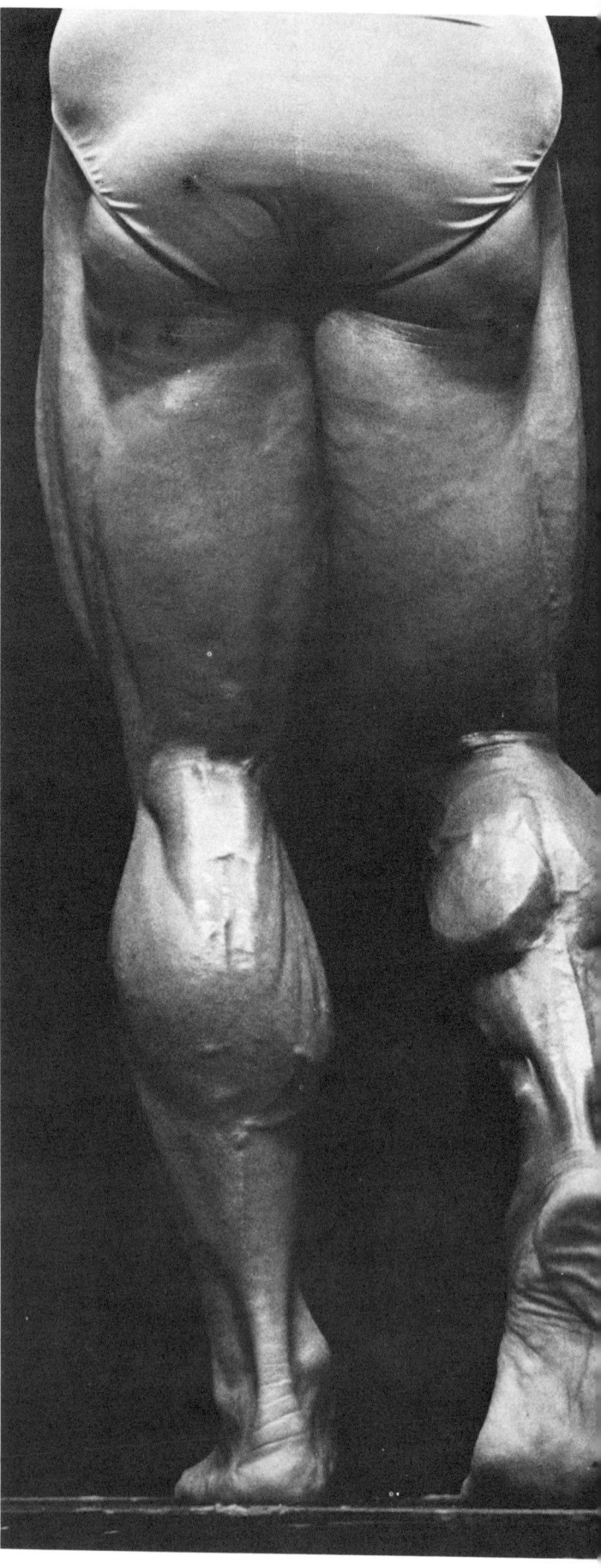

Improving your muscle mass, whether it be in your calves or arms, requires the correct balance of exercise and rest.

athletes, especially bodybuilders and weightlifters, are not deficient in protein. In fact, most bodybuilders consume at least three times as much protein per day as they need for maximum muscular growth.

The amount of protein you need per day can be determined by multiplying your bodyweight in pounds by .36 grams. For example, if you weigh 175 pounds, then $175 \times .36 = 63$ grams of protein daily. Most bodybuilders get more than 63 grams of protein in each of their three or four meals a day.

If you are dissatisfied with your present muscular development, there's a high probability that the fault lies not with your nutritional practices or lack of protein, but with the two most important factors: *exercise* and *rest*.

Split Routines

Q. *What is the problem with performing a split routine: working the lower body on one day and upper body the next?*

A. Many bodybuilding authorities have recognized that high-intensity exercise for the major muscle masses results in large-scale growth for those muscles as well as a lower order of growth in other muscles. Arthur Jones believes that this "indirect growth effect" occurs as a result of a chemical reaction. As a muscle works intensely, a chemical reaction occurs that spills over and affects the entire body.

Since there is a limit to your overall recovery ability, and since many of the body's chemical functions affect the entire body, it should be evident that training every day is a mistake. Even if a split routine is used, the system cannot recover from a hard workout in fewer than 48 hours. If a high-intensity lower body workout is done between each hard workout for your upper body, your overall system will never be given enough time for full recovery and growth. In employing a split routine you may believe you are only working your upper or lower body, but this is impossible because of the indirect effect.

Rather than using the indirect growth effect to your disadvantage, use it to your advantage. Instead of training every day on a split routine, train your body in an overall fashion only three times a week.

Every Day Arm Cycle

Q. *What would happen if I did the arm cycle every day for several weeks?*

A. If you reduced your other body-part exercises to a bare minimum to save your recovery ability, you might note some growth in your arms—at least for awhile. But within two weeks, you would also see the effects of atrophy occurring in the muscles that were not working

The muscular physique of Mike Watson.
Opposite, above. Jon Aranita does a set of incline flies.
Opposite, below. Ask Grizzly Brown about bench pressing and he'll set you straight.

183

intensely.

The most efficient way to get massive arms is by specializing on your arms two or three times per week for four weeks in a row (see Chapter 9). At the same time you should also work your other major muscle groups in a high-intensity manner.

Remember, overtraining is *not* the key to building larger muscles. Any amount of training is always a negative factor in that it drains some of your resources. The less you disturb your recovery ability, the more you will have available for growth.

Utilize the recommended arm cycle for bigger biceps and triceps. But use it prudently.

Number of Advanced Cycles per Workout

Q. *How many of the advanced cycles can I perform in the same workout?*

A. In Chapter 3 the following advice was given:
- *Do not perform more than two specialized cycles during the same workout.*

For example, you might employ the advanced arm and the advanced chest cycles on the same day. Even then, two advanced cycles on the same day may leave you in a state of overtraining.

The specialized routines for your major muscle groups are all designed to shock a body part into renewed growth. A suggested cycle should be combined with several exercises for your other major muscles but with the understanding that your total exercises for the workout should not exceed sixteen. In fact, you will probably get the best possible results if you limit your total exercises to fourteen or fewer.

The Treadmill to Nowhere

Q. *What would happen if I did the advanced cycle for my thighs, calves, lats, chest, shoulders, and arms all on the same day?*

A. You would join a large number of bodybuilders who are on a treadmill that leads to nowhere but gross overtraining. To accomplish such a workout, you would have to lessen the intensity of each routine. And lessening the intensity would mean that your muscle-building results would be slowed to a snail's pace at best.

The primary idea behind bodybuilding is to develop your muscles, not to see how much total exercise you can tolerate. Keep your exercise sessions intense and brief. Your body's overall recovery ability, and ultimately your muscles, will thank you for it.

Building Confidence

Q. *I'm still not sure with only sixteen exercises or*

Lori Bowen-Rice.
Opposite, above. For best results, do not train your arms more than three times per week.
Opposite, below. Keep your total exercises to sixteen or fewer.

sets that I'll be getting enough work for my entire body. Can I simply double or triple the sets that you recommend?

A. Sure you can double or triple the sets. But if you do, you'll be making a huge mistake. To do multiple sets means you have to reduce the intensity of the exercise. Reducing the intensity indicates that your growth stimulation will be poor at best.

Why not give the super high-intensity way a fair trial? Give it your best shot for three months. If you truly put forth the highest intensity of effort in each of the sixteen exercises, then I guarantee you'll never be satisfied with any other style of training. Your muscular growth in three months will be that good—I promise!

But as important as anything I've discussed in this book is the fact that you must have *confidence* in what you are doing. Confidence begins with understanding. You must first understand the basic principles of super high-intensity training, which are detailed in Chapter 3. Merely going through the routines is not enough, since your effort must be maximum. You must understand what's happening, and you must believe in your training.

Some bodybuilders naturally assume that only one set of sixteen exercises could not work for them. In a sense, they psych themselves out before they give it a fair trial. Usually, they add other exercises to the recommended training, or they perform a moderate-intensity version of the suggested workouts. Either way the final results are poor, and they in turn knock the system.

The keys to efficient and effective muscle building are *intensity* and *form*. And both intensity and form must be *understood* and *learned* before they can be *applied*.

Read and study the principles in this book until you understand and have confidence in them. Some of the principles can only be understood through experience—so be patient because it won't happen quickly. But it will happen if you give it time.

Soon you'll be approaching your high-intensity workouts with confidence. Your body will learn to thrive on your hard, brief training. And best of all, your muscles will grow at a faster rate than you've ever experienced in the past.

Confidence begins with understanding.

Conclusion

Look for ways to make your training *harder* and *briefer*.

Advanced bodybuilders should be clearly aware that super high-intensity training is a catalyst that initiates the muscular growth process. That muscular growth process takes place hours or sometimes days later. But for the eventual growth to occur, your system must be well rested, it must *not* be overtrained.

If you want to reach your full potential and if you want to achieve it in two years rather than twenty, then you must conquer your desire for overtraining. And at the same time you must search for ways to make your exercise *harder* and *briefer*. *Super High-Intensity Bodybuilding* is the way!

Correct application of the advanced techniques in this book, such as

■ Breakdowns ■ Negatives ■ Super slow ■ Pre-exhaustion ■ 1¼ system ■ Stage repetitions

will produce significant muscle-building results. And those results will come quickly, if you employ the methods wisely.

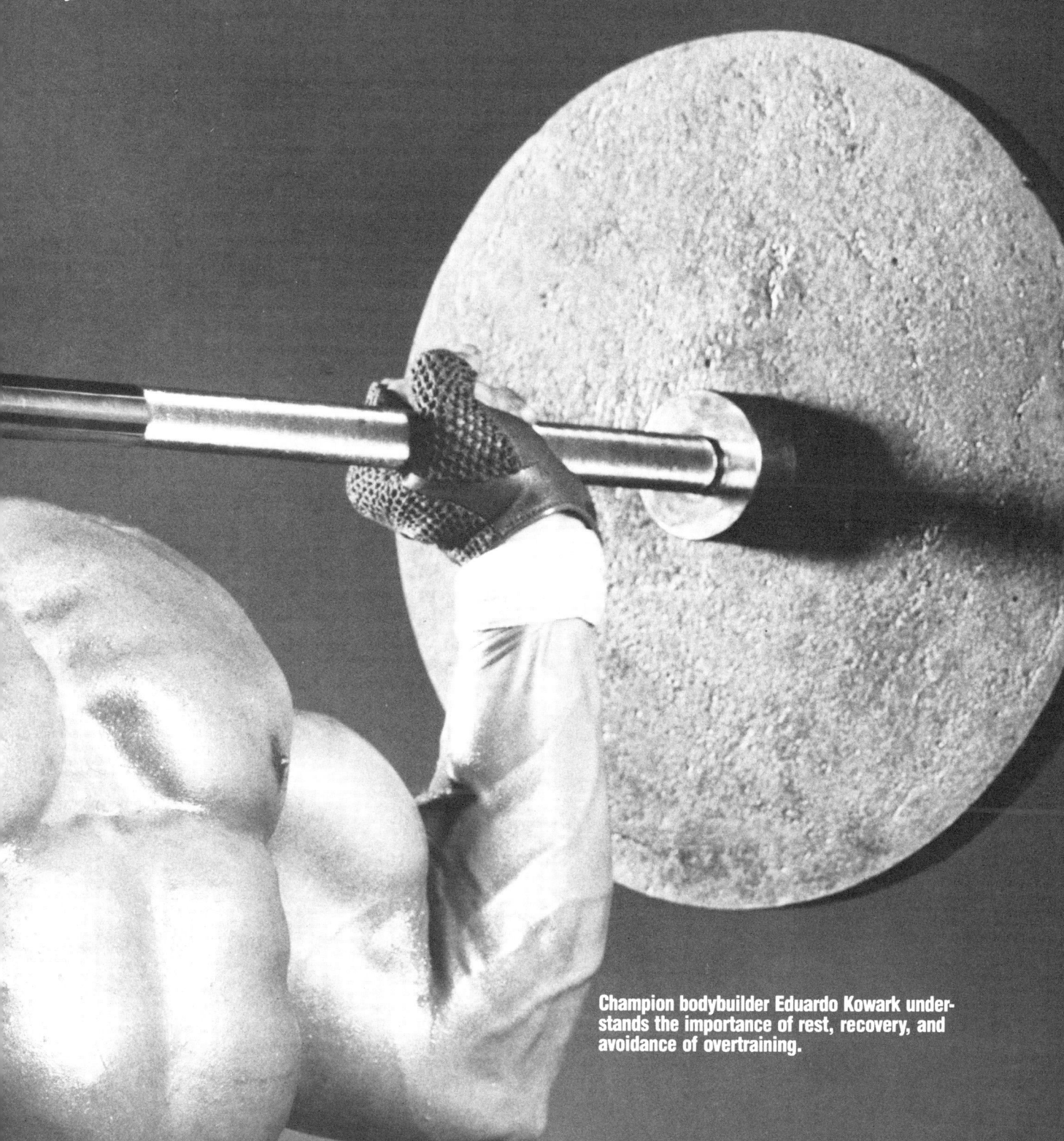

Champion bodybuilder Eduardo Kowark understands the importance of rest, recovery, and avoidance of overtraining.

Believe! *Super High-Intensity Bodybuilding* is the way!